Glass Candle Holders
of the Depression Era and Beyond

*Sherry Riggs and
Paula Pendergrass*

Schiffer Publishing Ltd ®

4880 Lower Valley Road, Atglen, PA 19310 USA

Designed by John P. Cheek
Type set in Korinna BT/Souvenir Lt BT

ISBN: 0-7643-1348-7
Printed in China
1 2 3 4

Published by Schiffer Publishing Ltd.
4880 Lower Valley Road
Atglen, PA 19310
Phone: (610) 593-1777; Fax: (610) 593-2002
E-mail: Schifferbk@aol.com
Please visit our web site catalog at
www.schifferbooks.com
We are always looking for people to write books on new and related subjects. If you have an idea for a book, please contact us at the above address.

This book may be purchased from the publisher.
Include $3.95 for shipping.
Please try your bookstore first.
You may write for a free catalog.

In Europe, Schiffer books are distributed by
Bushwood Books
6 Marksbury Avenue
Kew Gardens
Surrey TW9 4JF England
Phone: 44 (0) 20 8392 8585
Fax: 44 (0) 20 8392 9876
E-mail: Bushwd@aol.com
Free postage in the UK. Europe: air mail at cost.

Contents

Preface

Surely collectors in the United States have embraced the glass candle holder more than those in any other country. Variations in colors, styles, and treatments available in today's market are truly phenomenal. From the simplest votive to the most elegant candelabra, there is something for everyone and, importantly, there are delightful candle holders in every price range.

In this book we showcase an array of candle holders ranging from as little as $6.00 to as much as $1200.00 each. We have included representatives from the major U.S. lines, from small U.S. companies, and from numerous import markets. Whatever your taste, whatever your budget, there are plenty of choices to tempt you. So read and enjoy!

Acknowledgments

Collectors and Consultants

Tom Bloom, C.J. Bodensteiner, Al and Lib Davidson, Eddie Dean, Mr. and Mrs. Horace Dickens, Joy Griggs, Bill and Diane Haight, Tommie C. Hinski, Hanley and Margaret Jennings, Sim and Betty Lucas, Robert Meador, Armando Ramirez, Nancy Rowbottom, Janet and Dale Rutledge, Cheryl Sedlar, Gary and Janice Scheffel, Edna Staton, Nona Glass Taylor, Matzi and Jeff Thrasher, Mary Ann and Jay Thielen, and Enid and Len Waska.

Malls and Dealers

Bloom's Charles Street Antiques, Wellsburg, West Virginia; Han-Mar's Odd Shop, Weslaco, Texas; J.T. Texas, Tomball, Texas; Sherry Riggs Antiques, Houston, Texas; Sisters 2 Too, Alma, Arkansas; The Antique Company Mall, McKinney, Texas; Timely Treasures Antiques, Houston, Texas; and We Love Antiques, Dover, Arkansas.

Technical Support

Bill Belovicz, Ken Riggs, Mark and Bridgitt Ussery: Express Foto, Russellville, Arkansas; and Monica Romero and Stacey Landing: Eckerd Photo, Houston, Texas.

Editorial Support

The Schiffer Publishing Group and its staff; Peter Schiffer; and our editor, Donna Baker.

Introduction

This book continues our survey of candle holders available in antique malls and flea markets. We have included the major U.S. makers with additional Roaring '20s and Depression era candle holders with special treatments, cuttings, and etchings. We have also included candle holders from some of the smaller U.S. makers who may become the major producers of the twenty-first century. Imports make up an increasing share of the U.S. market for fine glass, and we have added Venetian and Czech candle holders as well as representatives from other foreign markets.

Identification of candle holders in this book is based on publications, catalogs, manufacturer's verification, manufacturers' marks, and affixed labels. **Pricing** is based on publications, mall prices,

glass show prices, and advice from expert collectors and dealers. Although our pricing research is comprehensive, it is not foolproof; it cannot account for regional differences, nor can it predict future trends. Prices are given as a suggested range for mint condition items, with the upper price being for the most desirable colors and/or treatments.

Candle holders are listed alphabetically by manufacturer or known retailer. For example, a candle holder made by Fenton for L.G. Wright will be listed under L.G. Wright with a note that it was made by Fenton. Foreign candle holders are listed by country with the manufacturer also being identified, if known. The progression in each section is from shorter to taller, and from single, to double, to triple; however, similar candle holders have been grouped by line number or by style in some places.

All measurements in this book are actual measurements of the candle holder shown, not catalog listings. **A word of caution**: candle holders from the same line commonly vary ± 0.5 inch, so a candle holder described in the literature as being 3" could be as short as 2.5" while another one could be as tall as 3.5". (Here's a **tip** from Sim Lucas: "if you don't have a tape [measure], you can use a dollar bill which is 6" long on the button!")

A **bobeche** is a ring placed or molded around the base of the light; **prisms** are generally attached. For consistency, we have used the term **candelabra** to refer to holders with bobeches and prisms attached. The term **lustre** refers to candle holders with a fixed bobeche; a **nappy** is a candle dish with a handle; an **epergne** is a vase that fits into the light in place of a candle. An **etching** is a roughened surface pattern usually created by sandblasting or the application of acid; a **cutting** is engraved into the glass with a sharp instrument.

Candle Holders
and Their Values

A & A Imports

St. Louis, Missouri.

A&A Imports 4.75" x 5" two-piece fairy light in overlay glass. Red cut-to-clear, blue cut- to-clear: $25-30 each.

A&A Imports
alternate view.

A&A Imports 10.625" 'Eiffel Tower' single light candlestick. Amberina: $20-25 each; ruby, cobalt: $25-30 each.

Avon Products, Inc.

New York, New York, 1939 to present. Formerly the **California Perfume Company** of Suffern, New York. Candlesticks and votives were made for Avon by several different companies. Perfumes, cosmetics, and toiletries.

Avon 2.875" 'Coral Glow' single light shell votive. Crystal only: $10-12 each. (1983-1984).

Avon 7.375" 'Opalique' single light candle holder. Crystal opalescent: $8-10 each. (1976-1977).

Avon (by **Fostoria**) 8.25" 'Washington' single light goblet votive. Cobalt with George and Martha Washington pattern: $18-20 each. (1975-1977).

Beaumont Company

Morgantown, West Virginia, early 1900s-1962. Tableware, boudoir items, and lighting.

Beaumont 2.625" single light candle holders, 5.5" single light keyhole style candle holder, and fan vase. Fer lux with flower decoration and gold trim: 2.625" candle holders: $30-35 each; 5.5" candle holder: $40-45 each; vase: $55-60 each. (1920s).

Beaumont 2" x 5.5" single light mushroom candle holders with flat rim. Black with silver triangle decorations: $40-45 each. Also comes with gold decorations. (1920s).

Boston & Sandwich

Sandwich, Massachusetts, 1826-1888. Pressed "lacy" glass, tableware, toy dishes, and lighting.

Boyd's Crystal Art Glass Company

Cambridge, Ohio, late 1978 to present. Novelty items in special colors.

Boyd 2.625" 'Swan' single light candle holder. Vaseline: $25-30 each. (1990s).

Boston & Sandwich 10.75" 'Dolphin' single light candle holder. Vaseline, amber, amethyst, electric blue, deep sapphire (also called cobalt), clambroth (white opalescent milk glass): $450-500 each. (c.1830-1888).

Brooke Glass

Wellsburg, West Virginia, 1983 to present. Operated as **Crescent Glass** 1908-1983. Hand painted lamps and novelty glass.

Crescent/Brooke 2" single light candle holders. Yellow satin and green satin with hand decorations: $20-25 pair.

Crescent/Brooke 2" single light candle holder. Amberina with floral pattern pressed on underside of base: $25-30 pair.

Bryce, Walker & Co.

Pittsburgh, Pennsylvania, 1855-1882. Became **Bryce Brothers** in 1882, moved to Hamondsville, Pennsylvania in 1889. Joined **U.S. Glass** in 1891 as Factory B. Moved to Mt. Pleasant, Pennsylvania in 1896 and remained until 1952. Ultimately became a part of **Lenox Corporation** in 1965 as **Lenox Crystal**.

Brooke 2.5" handled votive. Jade green: $10-12 each; ruby: $13-15 each.

Bryce, Walker & Co. 7" 'Fairfax Strawberry' single light lustre. Crystal: $80-85 each. First produced in the 1890s and continued into the early 1900s.

11

Cambridge Glass Company

Cambridge, Ohio, 1902-1958. Tableware, dinnerware, and occasional pieces of all kinds. The molds were sold to **Imperial Glass Corporation** in 1960.

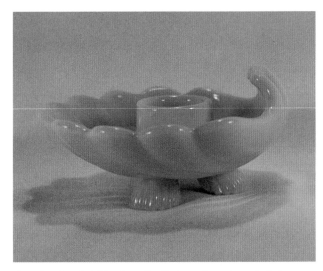

Cambridge 2.125" 'Sea Shell' three-footed single light candle holder. Windsor blue: $95-100 pair.

Cambridge 1.25" x 4" #2 'Star' single light candle holder. Moonlight blue: $30-35 each; crystal: $20-25 each; forest green (1930s): $40-50 each. Star #1 is 2.5" wide; star #3 is 5" wide; star #4 is 11" wide with a 1.5" candle hole.

Cambridge 3.25" #628 variant single light candle holder. Peach-blo with #725 etching: $55-60 pair. (c. 1930). The column ring in this variant is spherical rather than wafer-like. Used predominately in table centers.

Cambridge close-up of #725 etching.

Cambridge 3.75" #628 and #628 variant single light candle holders. The domed base shows etchings or decorations better than the flat base and seems to have been used more often for console sets. Crystal: $18-22 each.

Cambridge 4" #639 single light candle holder. Light emerald, amber, moonlight blue, peach-blo with cutting on base: $35-40 each; undecorated pastels: $30-35 each; crystal: $25-30 each; avocado opaque: $65-70 each. (c. 1920s). Also used for etchings and rock crystal engravings.

Cambridge 3.875" #628 single light candle holder. Crystal with unknown etching: $20-25 each.

Cambridge 4.125" #66 or #SS66 'Krystolshell' single light candle holder. Forest green (shown in 1940 catalog): $75-80 each; coral: $120-130 each.

Cambridge 4.375" #68 line #3900 'Corinth' single light candle holder. Crystal only: $30-35 pair. (c. 1930s). This candle holder has a large, slightly domed base and was frequently used for etchings.

Cambridge 5" #646 ring stem or keyhole single light candle holder with decagon base. Crystal with gold encrusted #752 'Diane' etching: $125-135 pair. 'Springtime' (satin series) colors, pastel transparent colors: $35-40 each; ebony, ebony satin: $45-50 each; crown tuscan: $55-60 each; carmen, royal blue: $90-100 each. (c. 1930-1953). Used predominately for gold encrusted designs. **Note**: This candle holder really got a workout! These colors and prices also apply to #648 with a round base.

Cambridge 4.5" #10 'Everglade' single light candle holder. Crystal: $30-35 pair; carmine: $80-85 pair; blue willow, forest green: $55-60 pair.

Cambridge 6.25" 'Calla Lily' candle holders. Emerald green with enamel and gold decoration: $55-60 each; undecorated: crystal, amber: $30-35 each; rock crystal, emerald, ebony: $35-40 each; light emerald, forest green, heatherbloom, moonlight: $70-75 each. (1949-1953).

Cambridge 6.5" #1596 single light base for 'Table Charms.' Crystal only: $25-30 each. Can be found with various treatments. Also made in 7", #1597; 8", #1598; and 9", #1599.

Cambridge console set with 6.25" 'Calla 'Lilly' candle holders and 13" #3400/48 four-footed bowl. Emerald green with enamel and gold decoration: $185-200.

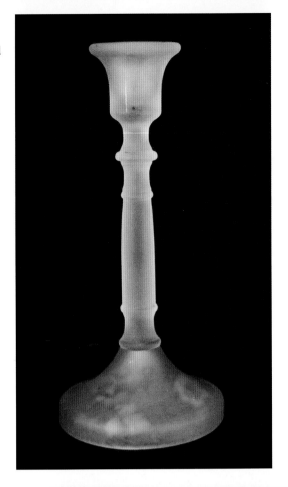

Cambridge 6.5" #73 "Reflector' single light candle holder. Crystal (c. 1945): $140-150 each; white milk glass (c. 1954): $125-135 each; moonlight blue (1941): scarce; cannot price. Introduced in 1941.

Right: **Cambridge** 9.25" single light candle holder. Crystal with etching and gold decoration: $35-40 each. **Lotus** purchased this blank for their #200 pattern.

Cambridge alternate view.

Cambridge 8.375" single light candle holder. Rubina (rare): $100-110 each. (c. 1925).

Cambridge 8" #50 'Dolphin' single light candle holder. Crown Tuscan: $250-275 each; white milk glass, crystal: $150-165 each; amber: $175-200 each. (c. 1930s-1954). Also found with a rim for bobeches and/or hurricane globes.

Cambridge 7.5" #3121 single light candelabra. Crystal with gold encrusted #D/1041 'Rose Point' etching and #D/1051 'Gold Edge' on bobeche: $135-145 each. (c. 1949-1953).

Cambridge 8.375" #3011 'Statuesque' or #61 'Seashell' single light candle holder. Crown tuscan (coral): $140-150 each; Windsor blue, crystal with carmen: $275-295 each; crystal with amethyst, crystal with emerald: $250-265 each.

Cambridge 9.25" #65 'Doric Column' single light candle holder. Transparent colors: peach-blo, amber, forest green: $65-50 each; crystal: $55-60 each; amethyst: $70-75 each; royal blue: $80-85 each; rubina: $225-240 each. (c. 1920s-1930s). 'Doric Column' was part of the 'Nearcut' series.

Cambridge 9.5" single light candle holder/vase. Primrose (1923-1925) with gold decoration and gold rims: $70-75 each; azurite (1922-1925); $65-70 each.

Cambridge 9" #1440 single light six-paneled candelabra with locking bobeche and 'A' prisms. Crystal only: $65-70 each.

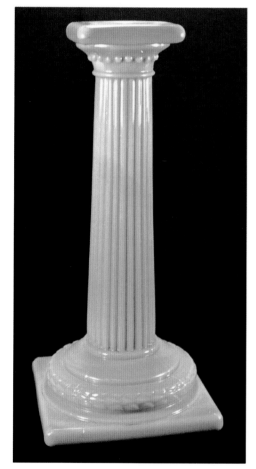

Cambridge 9.25" #65 'Doric Column' single light candle holder. Opaque colors: azurite, ebony, jade: $70-75 each; ivory (custard), carrara (white): $125-135 each; helio (purple): $165-175 each.

Cambridge 5.125" x 9.5" #3 'Everglade' or #1211 'Leafline' double light candle holder. Willow blue (Eleanor blue): $275-300 each; crystal: $150-175 each; carmen: $375-400 each; forest green: $200-225 each. (c. 1933-1945).

Cambridge 5.375" x 10.625" double light candle holder base for twin hurricane globes (#1890) or epergnettes (#1588 or #1589). Crystal: $70-75 each.

Cambridge alternate view with locking bobeches and 'C' prisms. Crystal: $120-135 each.

Cambridge alternate view of #1588 or #1589 (no center vase) or #1890 (twin hurricane globes).

Cambridge 5.75" #69 'Caprice' double light candelabra. Crystal: $125-135 each; moonlight blue: $250-275 each; alpine: add $10. (1939-1945).

Cambridge 7.75" #71 'Caprice' double light candelabra with locking bobeches. Crystal: $175-185 each; moonlight blue: $350-375 each; alpine: add $10. (1939-1945). **Note**: This candle holder has two small knobs rather than one large knob at the top center; it also has bobeche lips.

Cambridge alternate view.

Cambridge 5.375" x 10.625" #1583 epergnette with crimped top globe with 'Rosepoint' etching . Crystal only: $150-160 each. (c. 1940s).

Cambridge 5.875" x 8.25" #72 'Caprice' double light candle holder. Moonlight blue: $85-90 each; La Rosa: $95-100 each; crystal: $35-40 each; alpine: add $10. (c. 1940-1941). This candle holder has the original candle cups.

Cambridge 6" x 8.25" #72 'Caprice' double light candle holders. (1941-1954) crystal: $35-40 each; moonlight blue: $85-90 each; La Rosa: $95-100 each; alpine: add $10. This view shows two different shapes of lights. The candle holder on the left is a replacement mold (c. 1942) for the one on the right.

Cambridge 7" #1355 double light candelabra. Crystal: $80-85 each; moonlight blue: $175-185 each; alpine: add $10. (1939-1945).

Cambridge 7" #1356 double light candelabra showing bobeche rim. Crystal $135-145 each; moonlight blue: $225-250 each; alpine: add $10. (c. 1939-1945).

Cambridge alternate view with two #19 bobeches and sixteen #1 prisms.

Cambridge 5" x 8.50" #1307 triple light candle holder. Crystal with #754 'Portia' etching: $60-65 each; undecorated: crystal: $45-50 each; transparent pastels: $70-75 each; royal blue, crown tuscan: $140-150 each. (c. 1936-1953).

Cambridge 5.25" x 8.25" #1307 triple light candle holder. Amber with #E757 'Grape Leaf' etching: $85-95 each. This etching was introduced in 1932.

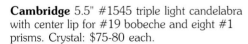

Cambridge 5.5" #1545 triple light candelabra with center lip for #19 bobeche and eight #1 prisms. Crystal: $75-80 each.

Cambridge 5.875" x 7" #1338 triple light candle holder. Emerald, moonlight blue: $80-85 each; La Rosa: $90-95 each; Mandarin gold: $65-70 each; royal blue: $125-135 each; crystal, white milk glass: $40-45 each. (c. 1930-1940). This is an older version with cross-hatching on the balls under the candle cups. Smooth balls were introduced c. 1939-1940.

Cambridge 6" x 8" #638 'Springtime' (special satin finish) triple light candle holder. 'Springtime' colors: jade (light emerald green), mystic (willow blue), cinnamon (amber), Rose du Barry (peach-blo): $145-150 each; Krystol (crystal): $45-50 each. (c. 1930s-1940s).

Cambridge 6.125" x 7" #1338 'Caprice' triple light candle holder. Alpine: moonlight blue: $85-90 each; La Rosa: $95-100 each; Mandarin gold: $60-65 each; crystal: $55-60 each. (c. 1939-1954). Note that the balls under the candle cup are smooth.

Cambridge 7" #1358 triple light candelabra with dark amber prisms. Crystal: $175-195 each; alpine crystal: $185-205 each; moonlight blue: $ 250-275 each; alpine blue: $260-285 each.

Cambridge #1573 triple light arm. Crystal: $60-75 each.

Cambridge 6.125" x 11" #1357 three light candle holder with #1573 arm. Crystal: $135-150 each.

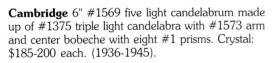

Cambridge 6" #1569 five light candelabrum made up of #1375 triple light candelabra with #1573 arm and center bobeche with eight #1 prisms. Crystal: $185-200 each. (1936-1945).

26

Cambridge 8.5" x 11" #1569 five light candelabrum made up of #1357 three light base, #1537 candle arm, #19 bobeche and eight #7 prisms. Crystal only: $195-210 each. (1940).

Central Glass Works

Wheeling, West Virginia. **Central Glass Company**, 1860s-1896; **Central Glass Works**, 1896-1939. Tableware, bar goods, and stemware.

Central Glass 2.875" x 5" single light ribbed mushroom candle holder. Amber, pink, green: $55-60 pair; with decoration: $70-75 pair. (c. 1920s).

Cambridge 10.75" x 13" #1568 'Caprice' five light candelabrum made up of #1457 triple light candle holder, #1432 candle arm, five #19 bobeches and forty #7 prisms. Crystal only: $300-325 each. (1940).

Central Glass 2.625" #2000 single light candle holder. Amber with cutting, pink, green: $25-30 each.

Central Glass 5.5" single light candle holder. Ebony: $50-55 each. This blank was decorated by companies such as **Lotus**.

Central Glass 7" single light trumpet style candle holder. Green with gold decoration, blue, cranberry; $30-35 each; vaseline: $35-40 each. (c. 1920s-1930s).

Czechoslovakia

Central Glass 5.5" single light candle holder. Pink with **Lotus** #204 'Sophia' line gold deposit $55-60 each; without decoration: $45-50 each. (1920s).

Czechoslovakia 2.375" single light cased glass candle holder. Mottled white, blue, and yellow light with green base, mottled orange, yellow, and dark brown with black base: $50-55 each.

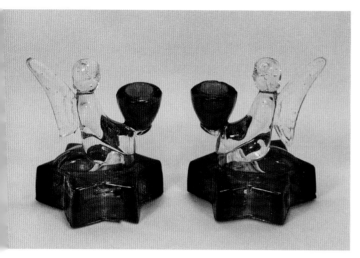

Czechoslovakia (Bohemian) 2.625" child's angel candle holders. Crystal with fired on cranberry $40-45 each; crystal: $25-30 each, Advertised in 1949 *House & Garden*. These have more detail on the hair and wings than U.S. versions. Originally sold in sets of four small or two larger candle holders.

Czechoslovakia (Bohemian) 7.25" Egermann type single light candle holder. Ruby cut-to-clear: $135-150 each.

Czechoslovakia (Bohemian) 6.625" single light candle holder. Crystal with ruby case cut-to-clear: $135-150 each.

Czechoslovakia (Bohemian) alternate view of cutting.

Czechoslovakia alternate view.

29

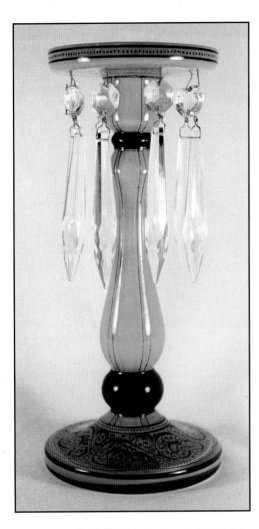

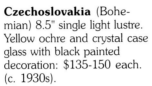

Czechoslovakia (Bohemian) 8.5" single light lustre. Yellow ochre and crystal case glass with black painted decoration: $135-150 each. (c. 1930s).

Czechoslovakia 9.25" single light candle holder. Blue with deep etching: $110-120 each.

Left: **Czechoslovakia** 9" single light candle holder. Crystal with fired on white and gold decoration: $75-80 each.

Czechoslovakia alternate view of etching.

Diamond Glass-ware Company

Indiana, Pennsylvania, 1916-1931. Tableware and occasional pieces.

Czechoslovakia 9.625" single light candle holder/vase. Crystal with orange and green fired on color: $75-80 each.

Diamond Glass 3" #99 single light candle holder. Yellow, black: $45-50 pair. (c. 1920s). Three-part mold.

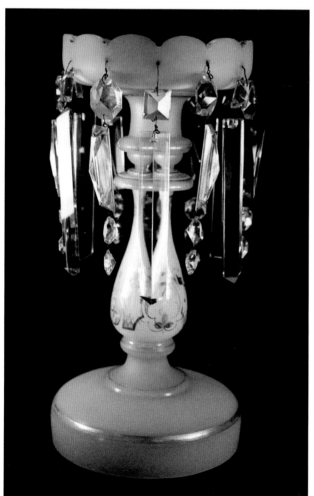

Diamond Glass 3.375" #99 single light candle holder. Black with silver 'Jack and the Bean Stalk' decoration: $45-50 pair. (c. 1920s).

Czechoslovakia 13" single light lustre candle holder. Jade satin with white opalescence and gold decoration: $200-225 each.

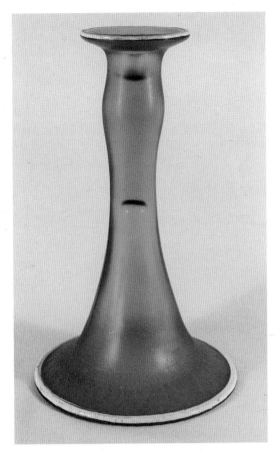

Duncan-Miller 3" #111 'Terrace' single light candle holder. Crystal with 'First Love' etching: $30-35 each. (c. 1937).

Diamond Glass 8.25" single light candle holder. Blue stretch with white enamel trim: $80-85 pair; cobalt with white trim: $100-110 pair; royal lustre with trim: $135-145 pair. (c. 1920s).

Duncan & Miller Glass Company

Washington, Pennsylvania, 1893-1955. Sold to **United States Glass Company** in 1955. The molds were transferred to Tiffin, Ohio. Dinnerware, tableware, and giftwares.

Duncan-Miller 3.0" #111 'Terrace' single light candle holder. Ruby, cobalt: $65-70 each; crystal, amber: $25-30 each.

Duncan-Miller 2.5" #153 'Contour' or 'Candlelight Gardens' or 'Tulips' three-piece table center with two single light candle holders. Dark green: $95-100 set; blue opalescent: $200-225 set; blue: $100-115 set; chartreuse: $80-85 set; crystal: $75-80 set. (c. 1940s). Reissued in the late 1950s when **Tiffin** acquired the molds. Greenbriar: $40-45 set; smoke $55-60 set; twilight: $100-125 set.

Duncan Miller 3.15"
#122 'Sylvan' single light
candle holder. Yellow
opalescent: $95-100
each; blue opalescent,
pink opalescent: $65-70
each.

Duncan-Miller 3.25"
#115 'Canterbury' single
light candle holder. Crystal
with 'First Love' etching:
$30-35 each. (c.1938).

Duncan Miller 3.25" #122 'Sylvan' single light candle holders. Pink opalescent: $65-70 each.

Duncan-Miller 3.25" #115 'Canterbury' single light
candle holder. Blue: $25-30 each; crystal, chartreuse:
$20-25 each; blue opalescent, pink opalescent: $45-50
each.

Duncan Miller #122 'Sylvan'
console set with 3.25" single light
candle holders and 4.5" x 12.5" bowl.
Pink opalescent: $225-250 set.

Duncan Miller 3.375" x 7.75" #30-1/2 'Aladdin' or 'Pall Mall' single light candle holder. Chartreuse: $35-40 each; crystal: $25-30 each.

Duncan-Miller 5.75" #28 single light candle holder. Cobalt, ruby, black: $30-35 each; crystal: $20-25 each. (c. 1940s). **Lotus** used this blank in pink, green, amber, ebony, and crystal. Also comes in 4".

Duncan-Miller 5.626" #155 'Festive' single light candle holder. Aqua: $100-110 pair; yellow: $115-125 pair.

Duncan-Miller alternate view. These candle holders come apart so that the mahogany disc can be oiled to prevent drying.

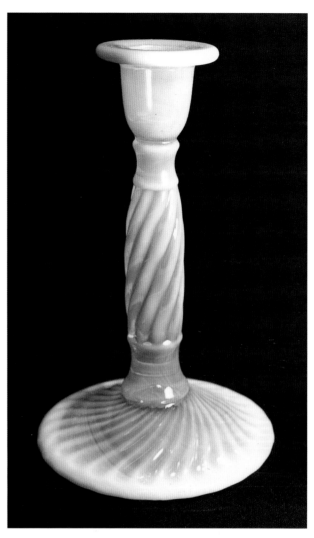

Duncan-Miller 7.75" #40 'Spiral Flute' or 'Colonial Spiral' single light candle holder. Blue opalescent, pink opalescent: $225-250 pair; green, pink, amber: $100-110 pair; crystal: $95-100 pair. (c. 1920s).

Duncan Miller 7.25" #112 'Caribbean' single light candle holder/vase. Crystal: $30-35 each; blue: $110-115 each. (c. 1935-1955).

Duncan-Miller #40 'Spiral Flute' or 'Colonial Spiral' console set with 9.25" single light candle holders and 11.5" bowl. Amber: $150-175 set.

Duncan-Miller 8" #36 single light candle holder, displayed on a 1.5" stand. Crystal with antique orange finish with black and gold decoration: $110-120 pair.

Duncan-Miller alternate view.

Duncan-Miller 9.75" #1-41 'Early American Sandwich' single light candle holder with bobeche. Crystal only: $90-95 each. (c. 1924-1955).

Duncan-Miller 6.5" x 7.75" #41 'Early American Sandwich' double light candle holder. Crystal only with 'First Love' etching: $45-50 each.

Duncan Miller 5" #41 'Early American Sandwich' double light candelabra with bobeches and prisms. Crystal only: $90-95 each.

Duncan-Miller 6.875" x 10.25" double light candelabra. Crystal with unknown floral cutting: $95-100 each.

Duncan-Miller close-up of floral cutting.

Duncan Miller 7.25" x 8.75" and 6.5" x 7.25" double light candle holders shown here for comparison. Crystal: $45-50 each.

Duncan Miller 7.25" x 12.375" 'Canterbury' double light candle holder and flower arranger. Crystal only: $95-100 each.

Duncan-Miller 6.5" x 7.25" #115 'Canterbury' double light candle holder. Crystal only with 'First Love' etching: $30-35 each.

Duncan-Miller 6.75" x 9" #41 'Early American Sandwich' triple light candle holder. Crystal: $65-70 each.

Duncan-Miller 7.25" x 9.25" #14 'Grandee' triple light candle holder. Crystal only with ' First Love' etching: $70-75 each; crystal without etching: $60-65 each; ruby: $250-275; cobalt: $350-375 each.

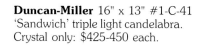

Duncan-Miller 16" x 13" #1-C-41 'Sandwich' triple light candelabra. Crystal only: $425-450 each.

Duncan-Miller 10" x 13" #1-B-41 'Early American Sandwich' triple light candelabra. Crystal only: $325-350 each. The company made its own prisms during World War II.

Duncan-Miller 9.75" x 13.25" #4 'Canterbury' four light candelabra. Crystal: $150-165 each.

England 2" single light press cut low candle holder. Crystal: $25-30 pair. Marked 'Stuart-England.'

England

England 1" x 4.25" square single light candle holder. Green: $25-30 pair. Part of a dresser set.

England 2.25" octagonal candle holder. Green: $35-40 pair. Part of a dresser set.

England 2.375" single light candle holder. Light blue with frosted swirls, pink, green, light ice blue: $30-35 pair. Part of a dresser set.

England 3" single light candle holder. Crystal with cutting: $30-35 pair. Marked 'Stuart-England.'

England dresser set with 2.625" single light candle holders, covered powder box, and tray. Amber: $70-75 set.

England 3.25" single light candle holders. Crystal: $15-20 pair. Part of a dresser set.

England (**Bagley**) 3.375" single light candle holder. Green flint: $35-40 pair. Part of a dresser set.

England 3.75" single light candlestick. Green flint: $35-40 pair. Part of a dresser set.

England (**Bagley**) dresser set with 3.375" single light candle holders, powder box, and tray. Pink, green flint, blue: $80-85 set.

England 3.625" single light candle holders. Green, pink: $30-35 pair. Part of a dresser set.

England 4" single light candle holder. Pink: $30-35 pair. Part of a dresser set.

England 4.5" single light candle holders. Crystal with frosted flowers, blue with frosted flowers: $30-35 pair. Part of a dresser set.

England 4.75" single light candle holder. Amber: $25-30 pair. Part of a dresser set.

England 4.5" single light candle holder. Crystal: $10-12 pair. Part of a dresser set.

England 4.75" single light candlestick. Crystal: $12-15 pair. Part of a dresser set.

43

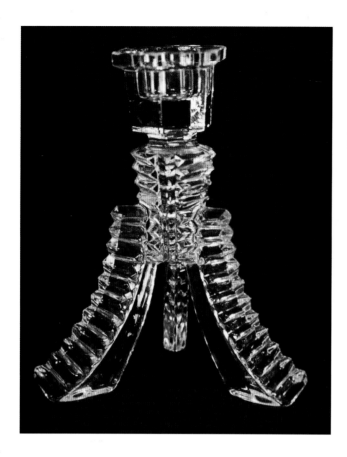

England 5.5" three-legged single light candle holder. Crystal: $30-35 pair. Part of a dresser set.

England 7.25" single light candle stick. Amber: $35-40 pair. Part of a dresser set.

England 5.75" single light pressed pattern candle holder. Crystal, amber: $20-25 pair. Part of a dresser set.

England 7" single light candlestick. Pink, crystal: $35-40 pair. Part of a dresser set.

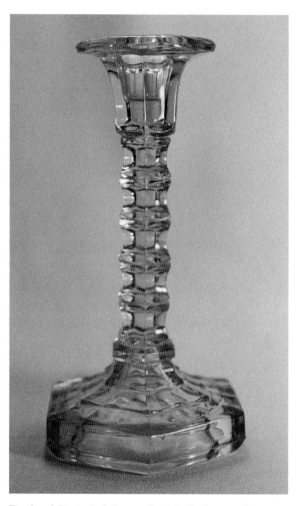

England 7" single light candlestick. Pink, crystal: $30-35 pair. Part of a dresser set.

Fayette

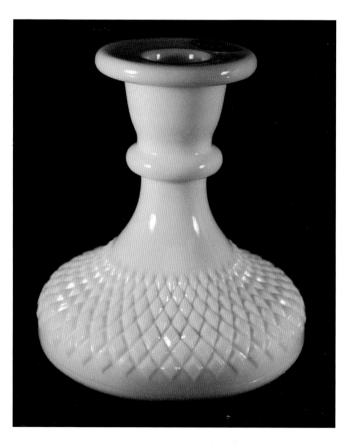

Fayette 4.25" single light candle holder with diamond press-cut design. White milk glass: $25-30 pair. Paper label. This candle holder is also found with an **L.E. Smith** paper label.

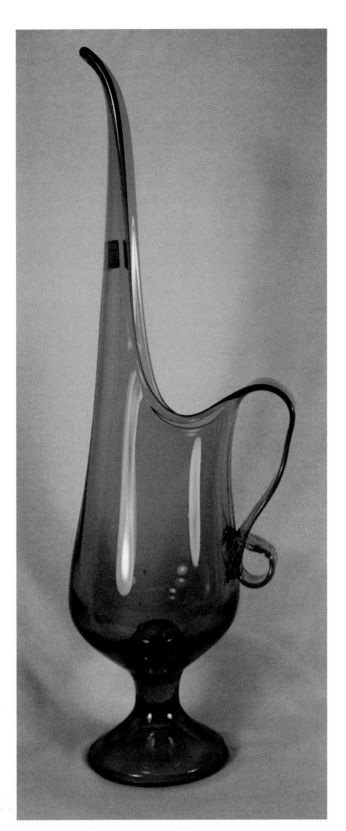

Fenton Art Glass Company

Williamstown, West Virginia, 1906 to present. Iridescent or "Carnival" glassware, art glass, and giftware.

Fenton 0.625" x 3" #9397WH 'Woodland Frost' pillar candle base. Crystal with icy iridescence: $10-15 each (c. 1999).

Fayette 16.25" single light blue candle holder/pitcher. Blue: $40-45 each. Paper label.

Fenton 1.375" x 3.625" candle holder/flower frog. Crystal: $10-15 each. (1990s).

Fenton 1.625" x 4" #848 three-footed single light candle saucer with snifter. Royal blue: $30-35 each. (1933-1936).

Fenton 2" x 6.25" #7695RU single light candleplate. Ruby, spruce, empress rose: $30-35 each.

Fenton alternate view with snifter.

Fenton 3.25" #9270 'Rose Pattern' single light candle holder in stretch glass. Velva Blue (c. 1981-1982), Velva Rose (1980-1982): $20-25 each. Marked.

Fenton 3.5" #8475 'Lily-of-the-Valley' single light candle holder. Pink opalescent: $50-55 pair; topaz opalescent (1980): $75-80 pair.

Fenton 3.5" x 8" #3771 'Hobnail' single light candle bowl. Topaz opalescent: $80-85 each. (1959-1960).

Fenton 3.50" #3974 'Hobnail' single light candle holder. Blue marble: $10-15 each. (c. 1970-1972).

Fenton 3.5" x 8" #3771MI 'Hobnail' single light candle bowl. White milk glass: $25-30 each. (c. 1959-1969).

Fenton 3.5" x 8" #3771 'Hobnail' single light candle bowl. Plum opalescent: $110-125 each. (c. 1959-1963).

Fenton 4.0" #38 'Vase in Hand' mini vase/candle holders. Celeste blue stretch (c. 1920s): $90-95 each; Opal colors (c. 1942-1944): topaz: $80-85 each; blue: $70-75 each; French: $60-65 each; spruce carnival (1999): $35-40 each. Also #5153 for **Levay** (c. 1981): purple stretch: $50-55 each.

Fenton 4.125" #377MI 'Hobnail' single light candle holder. White milk glass: $25-30 each. (1972-1977).

Fenton 4" (old **Westmoreland** 'Paneled Grape' mold) single light candle holder. Pink, green, blue: $35-40 pair. (1990s).

Fenton 4.375" #9372 (old **Cambridge** 'Gadroon' mold) single light candle holder. Red: $40-45 pair; ebony with copper rose decoration: $50-55 pair. (1990s).

Fenton 4.5" #1970 'Daisy & Button' single light candle holders. Orange, colonial amber, colonial blue, colonial green, crystal: $50-55 pair; blue milk glass: $55-60 pair; custard: $35-40 pair.

Fenton 4.875" #950 Cornucopia. Mongolian green: $55-60 each. (c. 1934). Notice the flat rim.

Fenton 5.75" x 4.625" #951 'Rose Crest' single light cornucopia candle holder. White milk glass with rose crest and hand decoration: $75-80 each. (c. 1946-1948).

Fenton 6" #951 single light cornucopia candle holder. White milk glass with hand decoration: $35-40 each. (1954-1965).

Fenton 6" #3874 'Hobnail' single light cornucopia candle holder. White milk glass: $35-40 each; French opalescent, blue: $40-45 each; blue opalescent: $50-55 each.

Fenton 4.875" #7300KE 'Jolly Snowman' single light two-piece fairy light. Cobalt with snowman scene: $50-55 each. Limited edition (c. 1999).

Fenton 4.875" #7300KP 'The Announcement' single light two-piece fairy light. Cobalt satin with 'Birth of Savior' scene: $65-70 each. Limited edition; part of an ongoing series (c. 1999).

Fenton 4.875" #7300GM 'Iced Pinecones on Gold' single light two-piece fairy light. Transparent gold with satin iridescence (called 'Gold Satin'): $50-55 each. Limited edition (c. 1999).

Fenton 4.875" #5405XP 'Violet Satin' single light two-piece fairy light. Orchid transparent with satin iridescence (called 'Violet Satin'): $55-60 each. Limited edition, part of the 'Historic Collection' (c. 1999).

Fenton 4.875" single light fairy lights.

Fenton 6.625" #7501TA 'Periwinkle on Blue Burmese' three-piece single light fairy light. Blue Burmese with white enameled beads and 22K gold: $175-185 each. Showcase dealer exclusive limited edition reissue of 1950 pieces (c. 1999).

Fenton 6.125" single light candle holder. Crystal with white iridescence with holly and snow decoration: $35-40 each. Signed.

Fenton alternate view.

Right: **Fenton** 6.125" #249 single light candlestick. Grecian gold stretch (crystal with marigold iridescence) (1920s), ruby (1925): $35-40 each; Florentine green stretch (1920s), Venetian red (1924): $45-50 each; crystal satin with 'San Toy' (1936) or 'Snow Fern' (1937) etching: $50-55 each; celeste blue, celeste blue stretch (1920s): $60-65 each; royal blue stretch (cobalt) (rare): $135-150 each; ruby stretch (1921) (rare): $160-175 each.

Fenton 6.5" #5172CN (carnival) single light swan candle holder. Black with iridescence (often called amethyst carnival) (1971-1973): $30-35 each; #6, Fenton Rose (c. 1938): $45-50 each.

Fenton 6.5" #1167 'Hobnail' single light three-piece fairy light. Red carnival (1994): $215-225 each; white milk glass with crystal edge on ruffle (1995): $85-90 each.

Fenton 8.125" #232 single light candlestick. Grecian gold (crystal with marigold iridescence): $60-65 each; topaz: $65-70 each; celeste blue, Florentine green: $80-85 each; wisteria: $100-110 each.

Fenton 6.5" #2903CR 'Heart Optic' single light three-piece fairy light. Dark cranberry opalescent: $175-190 each. (1996).

Fenton 7" #8406 'Heart' single light two-piece fairy light. Rosalene: $75-80 each; teal with marigold iridescence (1989): $65-70 each; wisteria: $45-50 each.

Fenton 10.5" single light hurricane lamp with etched bird on globe. Custard base with copper globe: $40-45 each. (1980s).

Fostoria Glass Company

Moundsville, West Virginia, 1887-1983. Purchased by **Lancaster Glass.** Dinnerware, pressed ware, and gift items.

Fostoria 1.5" x 4.25" #2402 single light candle holder. Rose, gold tint, green; $35-40 pair; crystal: $20-25 pair; amber, ebony: $30-35 pair; azure: $40-45 pair. (c. 1929-1939).

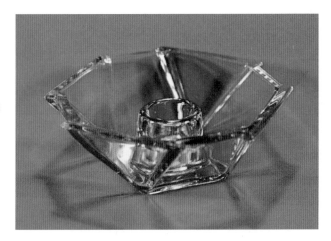

Fostoria 1.875" #313 'Glacier' single light two-way stackable candle holder. Green, brown, crystal: $10-12 pair. (c.1977-1980).

Fostoria 2.25" x 6" single light candle holder. Pink: $15-20 each.

Fostoria 2" #2545 'Flame' single light candle holder. Crystal (1937-1958): $20-25 pair; ebony (1953-1958): $35-40 pair; azure (1937-1940), gold tint (1937-1938): $45-50 pair. Also used with #26 candle lamp peg base and #26 candle lamp chimney.

Fostoria 2.25" x 7.375" #311 'Flora' line #2844 'Sea Shells' single light candle dish. Copper blue, green: $65-70 pair; crystal: $45-50 pair. (c. 1971-1973).

Left: **Fostoria** 2" #2430 'Diadem' or 'Crown' single light candle holder. Crystal with gold filled etching #575 'Richlieu'(1938-1939): $65-70 pair; crystal (1938-1943): $35-40 pair; ebony (1954-1958): $45-50 pair.

Fostoria 2.5" #2425 single light candle holder. Azure: $50-55 pair; green, rose, topaz: $45-50 pair; amber, ebony, crystal: $40-45 pair. (c.1929-1932).

Fostoria 3.5" #2592 'Myriad' single light candle holder. Crystal: $30-35 each. (1941-1944).

Fostoria 2.625" x 4.25" #2668 single light candle holder. Ebony (1953-1961): $35-40 each; crystal (1953-1964): $30-35 each. Also used as a base for a hurricane lamp with #2668 9" hurricane lamp chimney.

Fostoria 3" #2324 single light candle holder. Crystal with #56 'Antique' decoration and yellow/black base with gold rim; red/black; blue/red: $30-35 each. (c. 1926).

Fostoria 2.875" #2183 single light candle holder. White milk glass: $25-30 each. (1955-1958). Also used as a base for a hurricane lamp.

Fostoria 3.25" #2324 single light candle holder. Vaseline (canary): $30-35 each; crystal, amber, ebony: $15-20 each; green, rose: $20-25 each; azure, orchid, blue: $25-30 each. (c. 1925-1940).

Fostoria 3.25" #2324 single light low candle holder. Crystal with unidentified blue and gold decoration: $25-30 each.

Fostoria 3.25" #2324 single light candle holder with #305 'Fern' plate etching* and heavy gold edges (decoration #501 on ebony only, 1929-1932). Ebony with gold edges: $110-125 pair; crystal (1929-1934), amber (1931-1932): $70-75 pair; rose (1930-1934), green: $90-95 pair. *Etching dusted to show pattern.

Fostoria 3.25" #2424 'Kent' single light candle holder. Crystal only: $45-50 pair. (1939-1943).

Fostoria 3.25" #2324 single light candle holder with decoration #55. Green with orange tinted rings on base, various colors on crystal, amber, blue, and canary: $25-30 each. (1926).

Fostoria 3" #2390 single light candle holder. Rose amber (1927-1929): $20-25 each; green (1927-1929): $25-30 each; rose, azure (1929): $35-40 each; orchid (1927-1928): $40-45 each. Mainly used in console sets.

Fostoria 3.75" #2443 single light candle holder. Amber, crystal: $40-45 pair; green, rose, ebony: $45-50 pair; azure: $50-55 pair; wisteria: $75-80 pair; ruby: $90-95 pair. (c. 1931-1939).

Fostoria 3.25" #2362 single light candle holder with three-wafer center. Green (1927-1929): $20-25 each; blue (1927), orchid (1927-1928): $25-30 each. Also made in 9".

Fostoria 3.75" #2560-1/2 'Coronet' single light candle holder. Crystal only: $35-40 pair. (1938-1957). Also found with etchings or decorations.

Fostoria 3.375" #2298 single light art deco style candle holder. Amber with unknown cutting (used by several companies): $55-60 pair; without cutting: crystal, amber ebony; $40-45 pair; green: $50-55 pair; canary, blue: $60-65 pair. (c. 1924-1927).

Fostoria art deco three-piece console set with 3.375" #2298 candle holders and 7" x 7.125" #2324 footed urn. Amber with cutting: $140-145 set.

Fostoria 3.375" #2298 single light art deco style candle holder. Crystal with cutting: $50-55 pair.

Fostoria 4.25" #2630 'Century' single light candle holder with #342 'Bouquet' plate etching. Crystal only: $45-50 pair; without decoration: $35-40 pair. (c. 1949-1982).

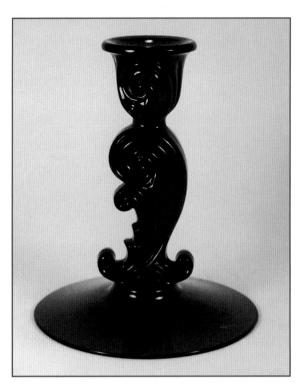

Fostoria 5.5" #2535 single light swirled candlestick. Regal blue (cobalt), empire green, burgundy, ruby: $65-70 each. (1935-1939).

Fostoria 4.75" #315 'Holly Giftware' single light candle holder. Ruby: $95-100 pair. (c. 1981-1982).

Fostoria 5.5" #2535 single light candle holder. Crystal with #325 'Corsage' plate etching (1935-1943): $50-55 each; crystal without decoration (1935-1940): $40-45 each. Used for various plate etchings.

Fostoria 5" x 12" #5056 'Heirloom' #1515 series single light candle/epergne bowl. Bittersweet (c. 1960-1962), yellow, pink, green, opalescent: $85-90 each; with epergne: $175-180 set. (1959-1970).

Fostoria 5.875" #319 'Heirloom' #2730 series single light candlesticks. Blue opalescent, yellow opalescent, green opalescent, pink opalescent, bittersweet: $45-50 each. (c. 1960-1962).

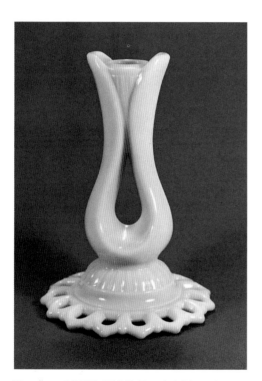

Fostoria 6.375" #2675 'Randolph' single light milk glass candle holders. Peach milk glass (1957-1959), aqua milk glass (1957-1959): $55-60 pair; white milk glass (1955-1965): $45-50 pair.

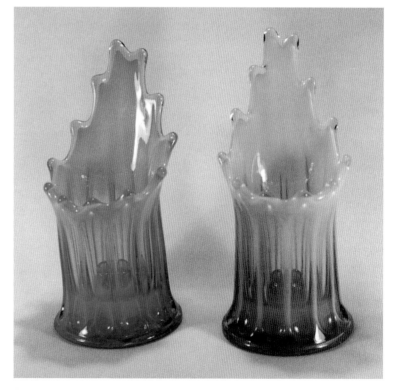

Fostoria 7.5" #311 'Heirloom' #1515 series single light candle vase. Green opalescent (1959-1961), pink opalescent (1959-1961), bittersweet (1960-1961): $80-85 each.

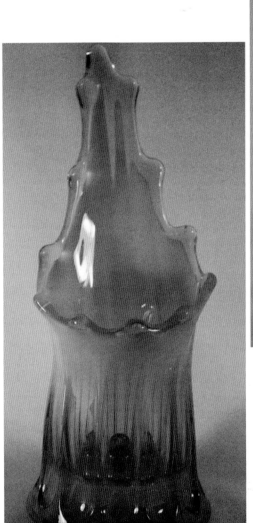

Fostoria 9.5" #311 'Heirloom' #1515 series single light candle vase. Blue opalescent: $80-85 each. (1959-1961).

Fostoria 8.375" #311 'Heirloom' #1515 series single light candle holder. Yellow opalescent: $80-85 each. (1959-1961).

Fostoria 7.625" #2545 'Flame' single light lustre. Gold tint (1937-1942): $75-80 each; azure (1937-1942): $80-85 each; crystal: (1936-1942): $70-75 each.

Fostoria 7.75" #2333 single light candlestick. Rose amber (1924-1928): $50-55 each; green (1924-1928): $55-60 each; blue (1924-1927): $60-65 each. Also in 11".

Fostoria 8" #2412 'Colony' single light lustre with 'U' prisms. Crystal only: $130-140 pair. (c. 1938-1959).

Fostoria 7.75" #323 and 5.875" #318 'Lotus Giftware' single light candle holders. Peach mist, crystal mist, ebony: #323: $50-55 each; #318: $40-45 each. (c. 1981-1982).

Fostoria 8" #2484 'Baroque' line #2496 single light lustre with 'U' prisms. Crystal (1946-1978): $55-60 each; gold tint (1937-1942): $110-120; azure (1936-1940): $120-130 each.

Fostoria 9" #112 'Cascade' single light candlestick with counter clockwise swirl. Crystal: $50-60 each. First produced in the 1880s. Reissued in 1926-1929 as #2412-9 'Queene Anne.' Crystal: $75-85 pair. Reissued in 1938-1979 as 7" #323 'Colony': Crystal: $50-55 pair; colors: $75-100 pair.

Fostoria 8.75" #2362 single light candle holder. Orchid (1927-1928): $60-65 each; blue (1927): $65-70 each; green (1927): $55-60 each.

Fostoria 9.375" 'Colony' single light candle holder. Crystal only: $75-80 pair. Part of the 1982 'Candlestick Collection.' Later called #319 'Maypole Giftware' (1981-1982): Peach, light blue, yellow: $140-150 pair. Also 3" #314 'Maypole Giftware' in colors: $90-95 pair.

Fostoria 10" #2777/327 'Rebecca at the Well' single light figural candlestick. Crystal mist: $95-100 each; olive green mist: $105-115 each; copper blue mist: $120-130 each. (1965-1970). Reproduction of an 1850 candlestick for the Henry Ford Museum. Marked 'HFM'.

Fostoria 4.75" x 5.875" #2424-duo 'Kent' double light candle holder. Crystal only: $65-70 pair. (1940-1943). Used before and during World War II for carved and cut patterns.

Fostoria 5.375" #6023 double light candle holder. Crystal with #12 'Morning Glory' etching on base: $150-160 pair. (1939-1944).

Fostoria 6.125" x 6.5" #2533 double light candle holder. Crystal only: $75-80 pair. (1935-1940).

Fostoria 5.5" x 8.5" #2694 'Arlington' double light candle holder. White milk glass only: $75-80 pair. (1957-1959).

Fostoria 6.625" x 8.25" #2533 double light candelabra with #2527 bobeches and sixteen prisms. Crystal only: $95-100 each. (1936-1939).

Fostoria 7" x 10.25" #2545 'Flame' double light candle holder. Light blue (1936-1939): $65-70 each; crystal (1946-1958): $55-60 each; gold tint (1937-1943): $60-65 each.

Fostoria 6.75" x 8.375" 'American' double light candle holder with bell base. Crystal only: $175-185 pair.

Fostoria 6.5" x 6.375" #2630 'Century' double light candle holder. Crystal only: $70-75 pair. (1949-1978).

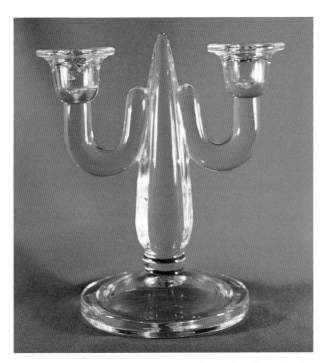

Fostoria 8" # 2598 double light candle holder. Crystal only: $95-100 each. (1940-1943).

Fostoria 5.125" x 7.125" #2547 triple light candle holder. Gold tint (1937-1939): $115-125 each; azure (1937): $120-130 each; crystal (1937-1939): $85-90 each.

Fostoria 8.125" #2601 'Lyre Duo' double light candelabra. Crystal only: $75-80 each (1941-1948). 'Lyre' was also made as bookends.

Fostoria 7.875" x 7.50" #2630 'Century' three light candle holder. Crystal only: $120-130 pair. (1950-1978).

Fostoria 4.625" x 7" #1546 'Quadrangle' four light candle holder. Azure: $120-130 each; crystal: $95-100 each. (1937-1939).

France

Portieux and Vallerysthall, both having originated in the 1700s, merged in 1872 to become **Vallerysthall et Portieux**. They separated in the mid 1950s and **Portieux** closed in the mid-1980s. **Vallerysthall** is still in production, but on a small scale.

France 2.5" single light candle holders. Crystal: $10-15 pair.

France ('Durand') 2.375" x 3.25" single light votive. Double cased blue and 24% lead crystal, ruby/crystal: $35-40 each. Marked 'G. Durand' on bottom.

France ('Crystal d'Arques') 2.50" x 4.75" single light bird votive. Lead crystal, 24%: $20-25 pair.

France 6.5" ('Longchamp, Crystal d'Arques') single light candle holder. Lead crystal, 24%: $25-30 pair.

France ('Crystal d'Arques') 6.50" single light candle holder. Lead crystal with cobalt drop: $25-30 pair.

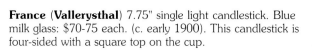

France (**Vallerysthal**) 7.75" single light candlestick. Blue milk glass: $70-75 each. (c. early 1900). This candlestick is four-sided with a square top on the cup.

France (**Portieux**) 7.75" and 6.5" single light candlesticks. Blue milk glass: $70-75 each. These sticks have identical patterns and have been rotated to show both views; they have lions on the base and round candle rims.

France (**Portieux**) 10.25" x 5.675" 'Bobeche Candlestick' single light candlestick. White milk glass: $95-100 each.

France (**Portieux**) 10" 'Bambous Ordinare, a Bobeche Candlestick' massive single light candlestick. Blue milk glass, white milk glass, amber, crystal: $95-100 each. (c. 1930s).

H.C. Fry Glass Company

Rochester Pennsylvania, 1901-1929. Continued production in receivership from 1929-1933. Purchased by **Libbey Glass** in 1933. Cut glass, colorful art glass, and "Pearl Glass" opalescent colored bakeware.

Fry 2.375" x 5" #3101 single light candle holder. Black with gold trim: $70-75 pair; azure blue with enamel: $85-90 pair; rose with gold: $70-75 pair; amber with enamel: $55-60 pair; royal blue without decoration: $75-80 pair; emerald without decoration: $80-85 pair; amber with gold: $55-60 pair. (c. 1920s).

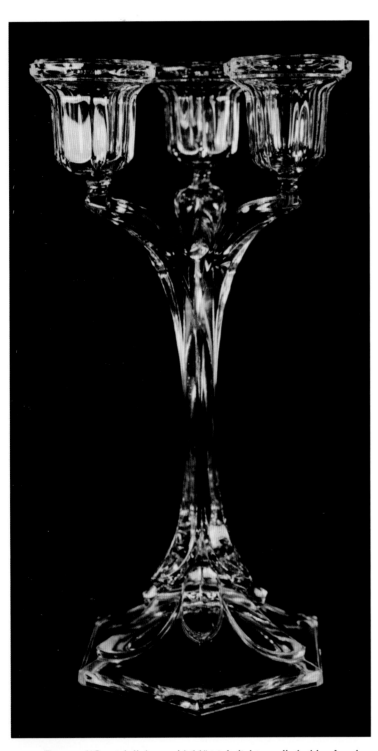

France ('Crystal d' Arques') 11" triple light candle holder. Lead crystal: $40-45 each.

Fry 3" #3101 single light candle holder. Rose amber with floral and gold hand decorations: $55-60 pair; rose with gold decorations: $70-75 pair; Royal blue: $75-80 pair; emerald: $80-85 pair; azure blue with enamel decorations: $85-90 pair. (c. 1920s).

Germany ('W.M.F.') 2.375" x 4.875" 'Starlight' single light candle holder. Crystal: $30-35 pair.

Fry 3" #3101 single light candle holder. Emerald with floral and gold hand decorations: $85-90 pair.

Fry 4.375" single light candle holder with crystal swirl connector. Royal blue: $125-135 pair; black, emerald: $115-125 pair. Note that the base is scalloped. (c. 1920s).

Germany alternate view.

Germany 6.75" double light candelabra. Crystal: $25-30 each.

A.H. Heisey & Company

Newark, Ohio, 1896-1958. Some molds were purchased by **Imperial Glass Company**. Elegant stemware and tableware.

Heisey 1.5" x 3.75" #99 'Little Squatter' single light toy candle block. Crystal with amber stain: $30-35 pair. Made for several decorating companies.

Good House Keeping

Heisey 1.75" #1489-1/2 'Puritan' single light candle block. Crystal only: $55-60 pair. Made from the 2.5" block by removing glass from the bottom then grinding and polishing top and bottom. (1941-1957).

Good House Keeping 6" single light candlestick. Amber: $10-12 each. This is a reproduction of **Boston & Sandwich** 'Petal & Loop.' Marked 'GHC' on bottom.

Heisey 2" #1507 'Lotus Leaf' crystal single light candle holder. Crystal only: $70-75 pair. (1947-1949). Used as part of a table center and as a base for the #341 epergnette. Some marked.

Heisey 2.5" #118 'Miss Muffet' single light candle holder. Flamingo: $55-60 pair; crystal: $35-40 pair; moongleam: $80-85 pair; gold opalescent (experimental): cannot price. (1926-1930). Also found with diamond optic base. Crystal is harder to find than colors. Some marked.

Heisey 2.125" x 4.5" #1632 'Lodestar' single light candle centerpiece. Dawn only: $125-135 pair. (1955-1957). Marked.

Heisey alternate view.

Heisey 2.875" #118 'Miss Muffet' single light candle holder with diamond optic base. Moongleam: $80-85 pair.

Heisey 2.75" #1506 'Whirlpool' or 'Provincial' single light candle block. Crystal: $35-40 each; limelight (rare): $400 + each. (1939-1944; 1949-1957). Reissued by **Imperial** 1960-1968.

Heisey 3.125" #1559 #1 'Columbia' single light candle holder with crimped foot. Crystal only: $85-90 pair. (1943-1944). Also made with #2 saucer foot that is harder to find: $115-125 pair. Few marked.

Heisey 2.875" #120 'Overlapping Swirl' single light candle holder. Flamingo: $60-65 pair; crystal: $35-40 pair; moongleam: $65-70 pair; hawthorne: $125-135 pair. (1927-1931). Some marked.

Heisey 3.125" #7000 'Sunflower' single light candle holder. Crystal: $45-50 pair; zircon: $400+ pair. (1938-1942). Not marked.

Heisey 3" #1566 'Banded Crystolite' single light candle holder. Crystal: $40-45 pair amber: $295-310 pair. (1947-1953). Issued as part of a console set and as a base for the #341 epergnette. Not marked.

Heisey 3.375" #1472 'Parallel Quarter' single light candle holder. Crystal only: $55-60 pair. (1935-1942). Few marked.

Heisey 3.5" #1533 'Wampum' single light candle holder. Crystal only: $50-55 pair. (1941-1942). There are two versions of this candle holder: the older version has a 3.5" octagonal rim; the newer version has a 3" rim and a thicker center post.

Heisey 3.375" #113 'Mars' single light candle holder. Moongleam with heavy cutting on top and base: $70-75 pair; without decoration: crystal: $40-45 pair; flamingo: $55-60 pair; moongleam: $60-65 pair; hawthorne: $125-135 pair; Sahara: $140-145 pair; marigold: $145-150 pair. (1926-1933). Some marked.

Heisey top view.

Heisey 3.5" #21 'Aristocrat' single light desk candle holder. Crystal only with cutting on base: $235-250 pair. (1922-1929; 1939-1944). Hard to find. Usually marked.

Heisey 4.25" #341 'Old Williamsburg' footed single light candle holder/epergne. Crystal only: $165-175 pair. (1945-1953). Marked. Hard to find.

Heisey 4" x 9.76" #1187 'Yoeman' or #1183 'Revere' candle/epergne bowl. Crystal only: $115-125 each; with 'Orchid' or "Heisey Rose" etching: $275-300 each. (1937-1944; 1950-1952). Few marked.

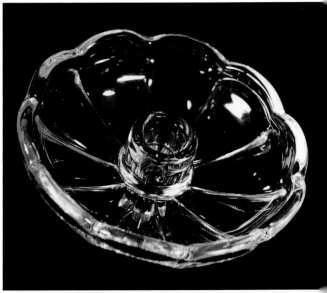

Heisey 5.5" diameter 'Old Williamsburg' epergnette. Crystal (1948-1957): $30-35 each; amber (c.1951-1953): scarce; cannot price. Marked. Also made as a saucer without the candle cup. Reissued by **Imperial**.

Heisey 4.25" #1567 'Plantation' single light candle holder. Crystal only: $110-120 each. (1950-1955). Usually marked.

Heisey 4.5" #520 'Innovation' two-piece single light candle lamp. Crystal only: $135-145 each. (1928-1929; 1941). Marked. The base, or well, was usually filled with colored sand or colored water; hence many found today are cloudy and will not command mint prices.

Heisey 4.375" #5 'Patrician Toy' single light candle holder. Crystal only: $90-95 pair. (1905-1931). Usually marked.

Heisey alternate view.

Heisey 5" #127 'Twist Stem' single light candle holder. Moongleam, flamingo: $245-260 pair; crystal: $120-130 pair. (c. 1929). Few marked.

Heisey 5.5" 'Patrician' single light candle holder. Crystal only: $95-100 pair. (1904-1933). Some marked. Also made in 6", 7", 8", 9" and 11". Reissued by **Imperial** in 1980, but renamed 'Squat.'

Heisey 6.625" #105 'Pembroke' single light lustre. Crystal with nine blue tear drop prisms: $235-255 pair.

Heisey 6.5" #105 'Pembroke' single light lustre with nine 'A' prisms. Moongleam: $220-235 pair; flamingo: $230-245 pair; crystal: $165-170 pair. (1925-1933). Usually marked. May be found with amber, amethyst, blue, or crystal tear drop prisms, or with 'A' or 'C' prisms. This is one of four **Heisey** lustres. (1924-1934). Also in 9". **Errata**: In our second book we stated that **Heisey** had made only two lustres.

Heisey 7.5" #28 'Elizabeth' single light candle holder. Crystal only: $110-120 each. (1908-1921). Some marked. Also made in 9" and 11".

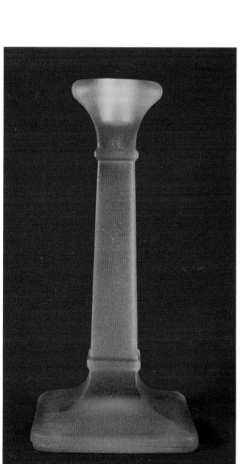

Heisey #1445 grape cluster single light candle holder. Crystal with #6 bobeche and twelve 'H' prisms: $245-260 pair; cobalt (rare): $1475-1550 pair. (1935-1944). Usually marked. May be found with 'A' prisms, 'H' **Heisey** prisms, 'P' prisms, and 'X' plastic prisms.

Heisey 7.5" #21 'Aristocrat' single light candle holder. Acid etched zircon (rare find): cannot price; acid etched crystal, crystal: $125-150 pair; crystal with full cutting: $300-325 pair; crystal with #9006 'Cairo' plate etching: $225-250 pair. (1907-1935; 1941). Most marked. **Note**: Zircon is not in the color listings for this candlestick. Since the top and bottom are not ground, we suspect that this candlestick was made by a worker.

Heisey 10.375" #107 'Wellington' single light candle holder. Flamingo: $275-290 pair; crystal: $170-180 pair; moongleam: $295-310 pair. (1925-1930). Usually marked.

Heisey 10.5" #1469 'Ridgeleigh' single light candelabra with 'A' prisms. Crystal only: $245-265 pair. (1935-1936; 1941-1942). Some marked. This version has a hexagonal skirted base.

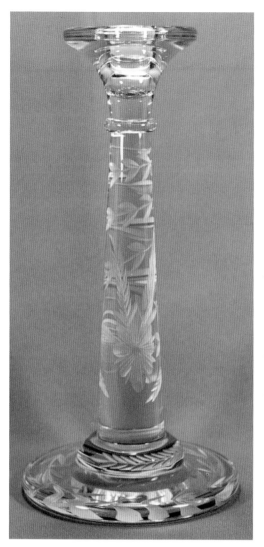

Right: **Heisey** 11" #20 'Sheffield' single light candle holder. Crystal with heavy cutting: $170-185 pair. Note the similar, but different, cuttings on these candle holders.

Left: **Heisey** 11" #20 'Sheffield' single light candle holder. Crystal with heavy cutting: $170-185 pair; crystal: $150-165 pair; crystal with moongleam candle cup: $265-280 pair. (1907-1931). Few marked. Made from two parts: a candle cup, and the column and base. Also made in 7" and 9", both in crystal only: $125-135 pair.

Heisey close-up of cutting.

Heisey close-up of cutting.

Heisey 12" #5 'Patrician' single light candelabra using a 9" candlestick. Crystal with #5 bobeche and candle holder, #54 ferrule, and twelve 'A' prisms: $450-475 pair; moongleam with crystal bobeche: $690-725 pair. (1905-1933). Few marked. Comes with 'A' or 'B' prisms.

Heisey 18" #400 'Old Williamsburg' single light candle holder. Crystal only with ten 'A' prisms on one layer only: $275-300 pair; with twelve 'C' prisms on lower bobeche: $375-400 pair. (1924-1944). Some marked.

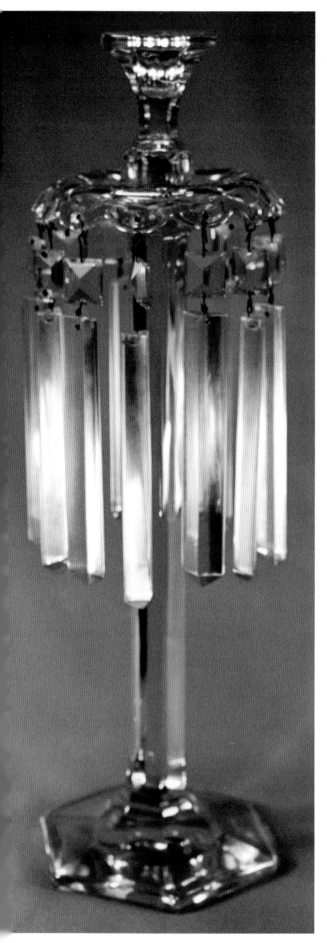

Heisey 19" #18 'Classic' single light candelabra with ' C' prisms. Crystal only: $350-375 pair. (1906-1924). Few marked.

Heisey 2.375" x 7.375" #1485 'Saturn' double light candle block. Crystal: $185-190 pair; zircon: $700-725 pair. (1937-1938). Few marked. Found with various cuttings.

Heisey 4.75" x 7.25" #1541 'Athena' double light candle holder. Crystal only: $120-130 pair. (1943-1948). Not marked. Made for Montgomery Ward as 'Imperial' (1942-1944).

Heisey 5.375" x 7.375" #1506 'Whirlpool' double light candle holder. Crystal only: $80-85 each. (1939-1945). Marked.

Heisey 5.375" x 6.5" #1433 'Thumbprint and Panel' double light candle holder. Flamingo, moongleam: $150-165 pair; crystal: $100-110 pair; Sahara: $160-175 pair; cobalt: $325-350 pair. (1934-1937). Usually marked.

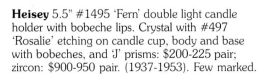

Heisey 5.5" #1495 'Fern' double light candle holder with bobeche lips. Crystal with #497 'Rosalie' etching on candle cup, body and base with bobeches, and 'J' prisms: $200-225 pair; zircon: $900-950 pair. (1937-1953). Few marked.

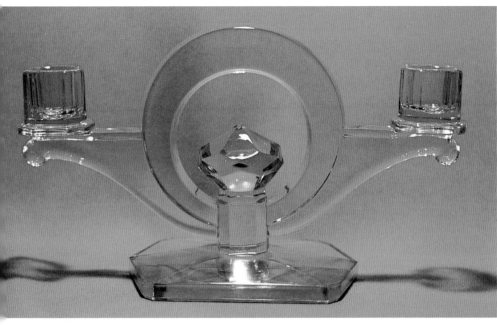

Heisey 5.5" #1488 'Kohinoor' double light candelabra with square bobeche with 'D' prisms. Crystal: $245-265 pair; zircon (scarce): $1600-1650 pair. (1937-1945). Also found with 'J' prisms. Offered without bobeches as a candle holder

Heisey alternate view.

Heisey alternate view

Heisey 5.625" x 7.625" #1951 'Cabochon' double light candle holder. Crystal only: $165-175 pair. (1951-1953). Marked.

Heisey 6.125" #1519 'Waverly' or 'Oceanic' double light candle holder. Crystal only with #507 'Orchid' etching: $185-200 pair. (1940-1953). Few marked. Used for several cuttings.

Heisey 6.25" #1425 'Victorian' double light candelabra. Crystal: $200-210 pair; Sahara: $295-310 pair; cobalt: $600-650 pair. (1933-1937; 1951). Usually marked.

Heisey 7" x 9" #1493 'World' double light art deco candle holder. Crystal only: $1150-1250 pair. (1937-1941). Few marked. Scarce.

Heisey 7" x 8.375" #1447 'Rococo' double light candle holder. Crystal with satin finish: $350-375 pair; crystal: $325-350 pair; Sahara: $645-675 pair. (1933-1938). Marked. The base is applied; Sahara is also found with a crystal base.

Heisey 10.5" x 9.5" #1615 'Flame' double light candelabra. Crystal only: $200-225 pair. (1950-1957). Marked. Used for various cuttings and etchings. Has an applied foot. Reissued by **Imperial** (1957-1969).

Heisey 16.25" #300-2 'Old Williamsburg' double light candelabra with twenty 'A' prisms. Crystal: $450-475 pair; Sahara: $825-850 pair. (1901-1944). Few marked. Note the linked crystal swag. Found with many different styles of prisms.

Heisey 7.125" #1519 'Waverly' triple light candle holder. Crystal only with #515 'Heisey Rose' etching: $200-225 pair. (1949-1957). Marked. Has an applied foot. Found with #965 'Narcissus' cutting and #507 "Orchid' etching.

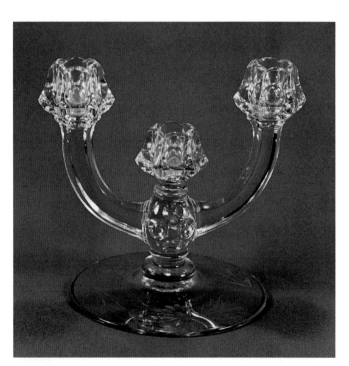

Heisey #1506 'Whirlpool' or 'Provincial' triple light candle holder. Crystal only: $95-100 each. (1938-1947). Few marked. Redesigned arms with small rounded waves produced 1948-1953. Both styles have an applied foot.

Heisey 7.5" #142 'Cascade' triple light candle holder. Crystal with #507 'Orchid' etching: $115-125 pair; cobalt with crystal base: $600-650 pair; Sahara: $250-265 pair. (1933-1957). Few marked. Has an applied foot. Found with various cuttings and etchings. Reissued by **Imperial** (1958-1968).

Henry Ford Museum

Detroit, Michigan.

Henry Ford Museum 2.75" single light candle holder. Teal: $20-25 each. Hand blown.

Henry Ford Museum 6.25" 'Sausage' single light candle holder. Cobalt: $35-40 each. Hand blown.

The Hocking Glass Company

Lancaster, Ohio, 1905-1937; became **Anchor Hocking Glass Corporation** in 1937 and **Anchor Hocking Corporation** in 1969. Still in production. Dinnerware, pressed ware, and gift items.

Hocking 2.125" x 4.375" single light candle holder. Amber: $10-15 pair. Marked.

Hocking 3.5" 'Cameo' single light candle holder. Green only: $55-60 each. (c. 1930-1934). Adapted from a **Monongah Glass Company** pattern called 'Springtime.'

Hocking 11" single light hurricane lamp with cutting on globe. Crystal: $25-30 each. Assembled by unknown company.

Imperial Glass Company

Bellaire, Ohio, 1901-1973. Sold to **Lenox, Inc.**, closed in 1984. Tableware, pressed ware, and slag glass.

Imperial 1.875" x 4" #1886/643 'Dewdrop' single light candle holder. Yellow opalescent: $20-25 each. (1960s).

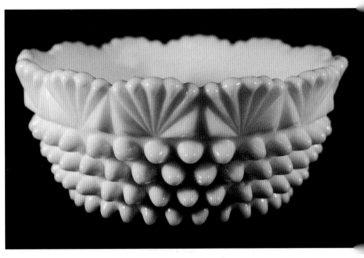

Imperial 2" x 4.5" #1886/643 'Dewdrop' single light candle holder. White milk glass, nut brown: $10-15 each; ultra blue: $15-20 each.

Hocking close-up of etching on globe.

94

Imperial 1.875" x 4.625" single light candle bowl. Blue, green; $10-15 pair. (c. 1970s).

Imperial 3.375" #1950/325 single light candle holder. White milk glass, doeskin (matte finish): $20-25 pair. (c. 1960-1973).

Imperial 3" #1155 'Aurora Jewels' single light three-footed candle holder. Cobalt iridescent: $25-30 each; white carnival: $20-25 each. (c. 1970s). Adapted from a **Cambridge** 'Everglades' mold.

Imperial 3.5" #708 'Twisted Optic' single light candle holder with swirl base. Crystal with hand decoration: $25-30 pair. (c. 1920s).

Imperial (from a **Heisey** mold) 5.125" 'Fish Candlestick' single light candle holder. Sunshine yellow: $35-40 each; sunshine yellow satin: $30-35 each. (c. 1982). Marked 'IG'.

Imperial 3.5" #160 'Rose' single light candle holder. Smoke iridescent, blue satin, amethyst carnival, sunburst (yellow), white carnival, pink carnival, horizon blue, meadow green: $20-25 each. (c. 1970s-early 1980s).

Imperial 3.5" single light candle/frog. Amethyst: $30-35 each. Marked 'IG'.

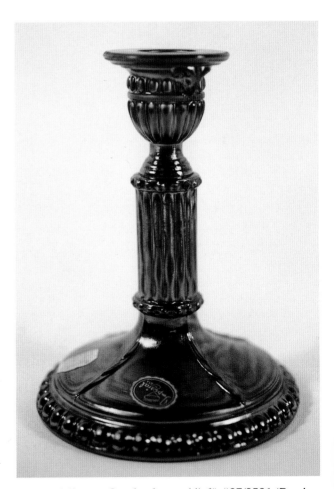

Imperial (from a **Cambridge** mold) 6" #27/3531 'Ram's Head' single light candle holder. Aurora Jewels (blue iridescent): $65-70 pair. Marked on base. (c. 1971-1972).

Imperial 7.375" #80 'Vinelf' single light candle holder. Turquoise blue milk glass, green milk glass, custard milk glass: $55-60 pair; white milk glass, doeskin: $45-50 pair; black with gold decoration, black suede: $70-75 pair; transparent satin colors: antique blue, cranberry: $40-45 pair; verde, crystal: $35-40 pair. (1950-1965). The mold was purchased by **L.E. Smith**.

Imperial 5" #169 double light candle holder with design under bottom. Ritz blue: $75-80 pair; crystal: $45-50 pair. Used in console sets with #648 and #656 bowls. (c. 1920s).

Imperial 4.375" 'Washington' double light candle holder. Brown, green, amberina, cobalt, black, crystal: $25-30 each. Introduced in 1920s.

Imperial 7.25" x 8" #75 triple light candle holder. Ruby: $75-80 each; crystal: $60-65 each.

Indiana Glass Company

Dunkirk, Indiana, 1907 to present. Tableware and gift items.

Indiana 2" 'American Whitehall' single light candle nappy. Crystal: $8-10 each.

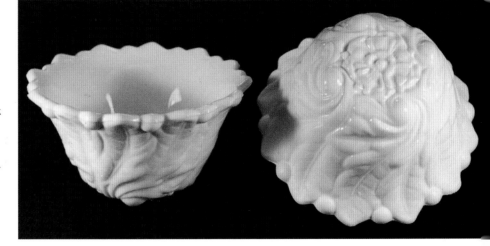

Indiana 3" 'Wild Rose with Leaves and Berries' single light candle dish. White milk glass, crystal, crystal satin, marigold iridescent: $10-15 pair; applied colors, satin colors with iridescence: $15-20 pair; multi-colored: $35-40 pair. (1950s-1980s).

Indiana 2.125" 'American Whitehall' three-footed candle bowl. Crystal: $8-10 each.

Indiana 3.125" x 3.875" 'Kings Crown' single light footed candle dish (**U.S. Glass/Tiffin** #4016 'Thumbprint' mold). Crystal with fired on cranberry: $30-35 each; crystal with fired on blue, crystal with fired on gold: $25-30 each. (c. 1970s).

Indiana 3.875" 'Oleander' or 'Magnolia' single light two-handled candle holder. Crystal: $25-30 each. (c. 1930s). Better glass sold in department stores during the Depression Era.

Indiana 4.125" 'Pineapple' single light candle holders. Yellow, amberina, crystal, blue, white milk glass: $15-20 pair; ruby (**Tiara**): $20-25 pair. (1980s).

Indiana 5.375" 'Diamond Point' fairy light. Blue, crystal, amber, amber with fired on red, frosted pastels: $15-20 each.

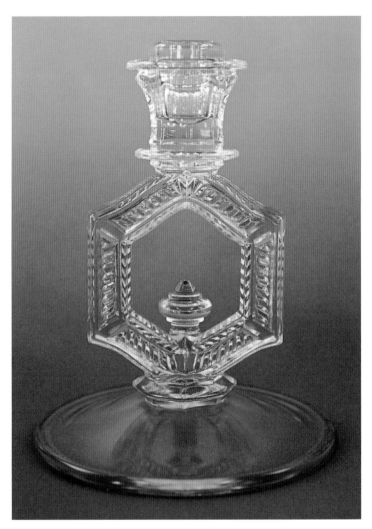

Indiana 6" single light key hole candle holder. Crystal: $20-25 each. Note the bobeche lip.

Indiana 5.375" 'Diamond Point' fairy light. Frosted pastel green: $15-20 each.

Indiana 7.626" (**Cambridge** blank) single light candlestick. Crystal with fired on green, crystal with fired on red-orange, crystal with fired on blue: $15-20 each. (c. 1920s).

Indiana 8.25" #6869 line #214 single light candlestick. Crystal: $20-25 each. Note the bobeche lip.

Indiana 8.5" 'Grape & Leaf' single light candle holder with hobnail globe. White milk glass: $45-50 pair. This has been assembled from a sherbet and a globe by an unknown company. It was found completely filled with candle.

Indiana 8.5" single light candlestick. Crystal with blue painted body and black rings: $75-80 pair; amber: $110-120 pair. (1920s-1930s). Three-part mold. Reissued for **Tiara Exclusives** in azure blue: $45-50 pair.

Indiana 5.25" 'Dewdrop' double light candle holder. Crystal: $55-60 pair. (1930s).

Indiana 5.375" double light candle holder. Crystal with blue cut-to-clear, crystal: $35-40 each. Note the bobeche lip.

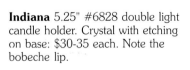

Indiana 5.25" #6828 double light candle holder. Crystal with etching on base: $30-35 each. Note the bobeche lip.

Indiana 6.5" 'Teardrop' double light candle holder. Crystal: $20-25 each; crystal with red flashed accents: $25-30 each.

Italy (Venetian) 3" single light chamber stick with lily base. Blue light with crystal and gold base: $90-95 each. **Note**: Gold leaf chips were added to hot glass then worked to create the crystal with gold effect.

Italy

Italy 1.625" x 1.25" miniature birthday candelabra. Multicolor: $35-40 each.

Italy 4" (Venetian) single light candle holder. Crystal with marbled cranberry leaves and crystal and gold feet: $95-100 each.

Italy (Venetian) 4.5" single light candle holder. Light blue opaque and crystal and gold flecks: $85-90 each.

Italy 6.25" single light handled candlestick. Green art glass: $45-50 each.

Italy (Venetian) 5" single light dolphin candle holder. Green iridescent and gold candle cup and base with crystal and gold dolphin: $250-275 each.

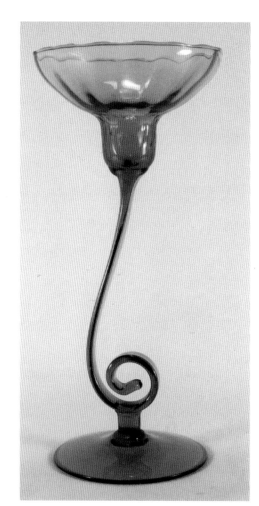

Right: **Italy** 7" single light optic candlestick. Teal: $45-50 each

Far right: **Italy** 7" single light optic candlestick. Amber: $45-50 each.

Italy (Venetian) 7.25" single light swan candle holder. Red with crystal and gold swan: $375-425 each.

Italy (Venetian) console set with 7.25" single light swan candle holders and 8.25" x 7" optic bowl. Red with crystal and gold swans: $1100-1200 set.

 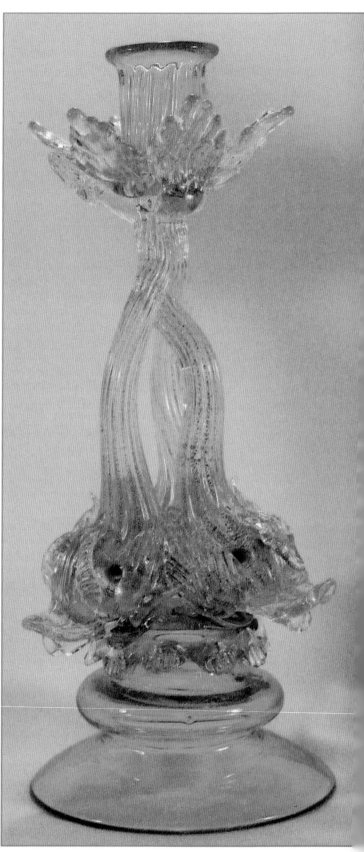

Italy (Venetian) 8.25" 'Dolphin' single light candle holder. Blue with gold fleck: $400-450 each.

Italy (Venetian) 9" single light dolphin candle holder. Crystal and blue with three gold dolphins: $225-250 pair. Both the base and the candle cup are applied.

Italy 8" single light candle/vase.
Green: $15-20 each.

Italy 9" single light candle/vase.
Green: $20-25 each.

Italy 12" single light candle/vase.
Green: $30-35 each.

Italy (Venetian) close-up of glass flowers

Italy (Venetian) 11.25" single light candlestick. Cobalt with gold streaks and glass flowers: $400-450 each.

Italy (Venetian) 10.75" triple light candle stick with glass finial. Blue with multicolored flower finial: $300-325 each.

Italy 9.75" single light candle holder. Rose satin candle bowl on crystal stem and base with silver metal rose on base: $135-145 each. Stamped '1993 Florence.'

Jeannette Glass Company

Jeannette, Pennsylvania, 1889-1983. Pressed ware.

Jeannette 2.625" single light candle holder used as the base for 'Cosmos'. Crystal with gold or silver-reflective rim: $20-25 pair. (c. 1950s).

Italy close-up of glass finial.

Kanawha Glass Company

Dunbar, West Virginia (old **Dunbar Glass Co**.), 1955-1988. Purchased by **Raymond Dereume Glass Co**. in 1988. Decorative wares, crackle glass, and case glass.

Jeannette 10.75" 'Cosmos' single light low candle holder and pegged hurricane light/vase insert. Crystal with white enamel: $25-30 each; marigold iridescent with white enamel: $30-35 each. (c. 1950s).

Kanawha 4" #850ED 'End of Day Glass' single light candle holder. Red slag glass, pastel blue slag glass, pastel green slag glass: $25-30 each. (1971-1973).

Jeannette 8" #5198 single light candlestick. Crystal with marigold iridescence, amber: $35-30 each. (1920s). Part of #X-30 buffet set.

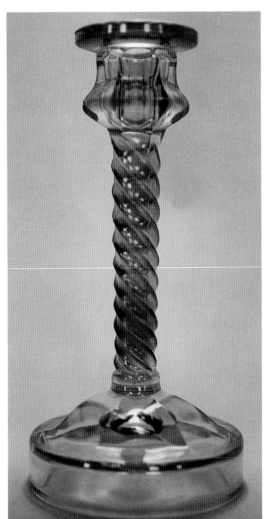

John E. Kemple Glass Works

East Palestine, Ohio, 1945-1970. Milk glass, pressed glass, and novelties.

Lancaster Glass Company

Lancaster, Ohio, 1908-1924. Became a subsidiary of **Hocking Glass Company** and continues production. Cut and decorated tableware.

Lancaster 1.5" dogwood single light candle block. Crystal with fired on color: pink, blue, frosted crystal, red, lilac: $10-15 each. Used in table centers.

Lancaster 1.75" x 7.25" dogwood single light candle block. Crystal with satin flowers: $25-30 each. Used in table centers.

Kemple (from a **Gillinder & Sons** #7 mold) 10" 'Crucifix' single light candlestick. White milk glass: $250-275 each. A similar smaller, less detailed mold was also marketed by **Kemple**.

Lancaster 1.875" dogwood double light candle block. Crystal with fired on colors: pink, amethyst, blue with gold centers, red with gold centers: $30-35 each.

Lancaster 2.5" #355 single light candle holder. Topaz, green: $30-35 pair. (c. 1932).

Lancaster 3" #854 single light candle holder. Vaseline with black enamel and gold trim: $40-45 pair. (c. 1920s).

Lancaster 2.75" #833 single light candle holder. Yellow with etching: $75-80 each.

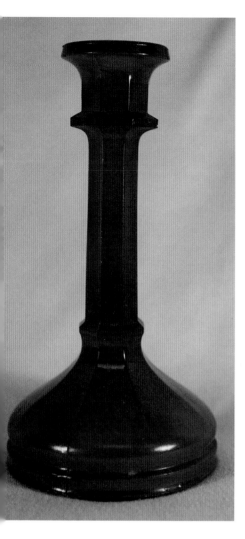

Lancaster 7" #85 single light candlestick. Crystal with fired on paint: blue, green, orange, yellow: $25-30 pair. (c. 1920s).

Lancaster 6.875" #85 single light candle holder. Crystal with fired on red-orange paint: $25-30 pair. (c. 1920s).

Lancaster 6.875" #85 single light candle holder. Crystal with fired on green and black: $25-30 pair. (c. 1920s).

Lancaster 7.5" single light candle holder. Light blue stain: $45-50 pair. (1920s).

Lancaster 7.375" single light candle holder. Crystal with marigold iridescence: $45-50 pair. (c. 1920s).

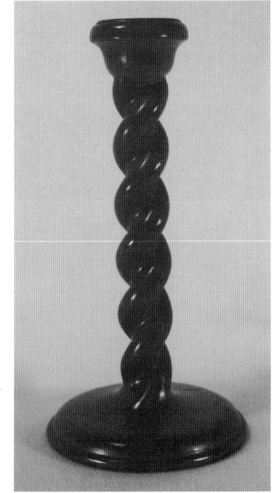

Lancaster 7.625" single light twist candle holder. Crystal with orange paint: $30-35 pair. Four-part mold.

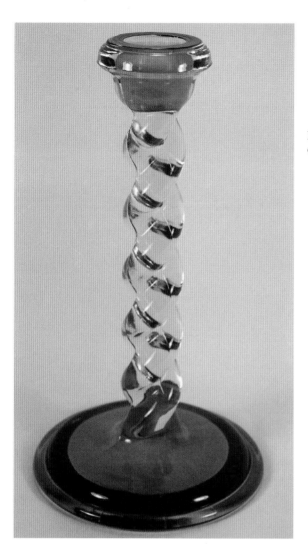

Lancaster 7.625" twist single light
candle holder. Green/black: $30-35 pair.

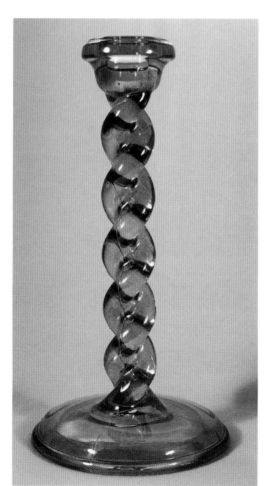

Lancaster 8.375" #984 single light candle holder. Pink
with heavy silver deposit: $70-75 pair; crystal with fired
on colors: $35-30 pair.

Lancaster 7.625" twist single light candle
holder. Crystal with blue stain: $30-35 pair.

Lenox, Inc.

L.E. Smith Glass Company

Mt. Pleasant, Pennsylvania, 1907 to present. Black glass.

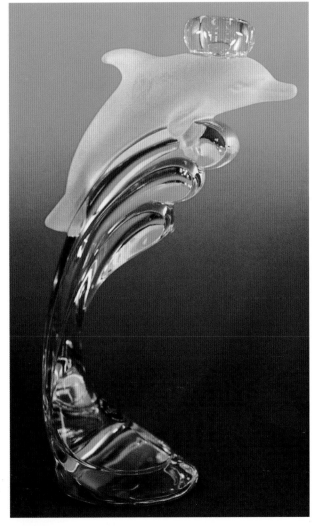

Lenox 2.25" x 6.125" single light bird candle holder. Crystal: $10-15 each. Paper label.

L.E. Smith 2.375" #27 single light candle holder. White milk glass with black ring decorations: $8-10 each.

L.E. Smith 2.375" #27 single light candle holder. Cobalt: $15-20 each.

Lenox 9.125" single light dolphin candlestick. Crystal/crystal satin: $25-30 each. Marked. Made in Germany.

Liberty Works

Egg Harbor, New Jersey, c. 1914-1932. Destroyed by fire. Started in 1903 as **Liberty Cut Glass Works**. Tableware, stemware, cut, etched, and decorated glass; unusual two-tone color combinations.

L.E. Smith 7.5" #4 'Almond Nouveau Collection' single light candlestick. Milk glass with caramel and beige slag: $25-30 each

Liberty Works 3.375" single light candle holder. Green, pink: $35-40 pair; crystal: $25-30 pair.

Liberty Works 3.25" x 5" single light candle holder with hexagonal base. Rose with cutting on base, green: $35-40 pair; crystal: $25-30 pair. (1920s). Note the double ring on the stem. Compare with **McKee** #200.

117

Liberty Works 3.25" x 5" single light candle holder with hexagonal base. Green with cutting on base: $35-40 pair.

McKee 3.25" x 4.25" single light candle holder with diamond and thumbprint design. White milk glass, crystal: $45-50 pair. Very similar to **Imperial** 'Cape Cod' pattern.

McKee Glass Company

Jeannette, Pennsylvania, 1900 to 1951. Tableware, kitchen ware, and gift items.

McKee 2.5" x 4.75" #154 line #2 mushroom style single light candle holder. Rose pink with etching: $60-65 pair.

McKee alternate view.

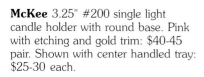

McKee 3.25" #200 single light candle holder with round base. Pink with etching and gold trim: $40-45 pair. Shown with center handled tray: $25-30 each.

McKee 3.25" #200 single light candle holder with hexagonal base. Pink with cutting: $45-50 pair.

McKee close-up of etching.

McKee 4.125" 'Autumn' single light candle holder. Jade green, French ivory: $60-65 pair; white opal: $45-50 pair. (1934).

Mexico

Mexico 4.875" single light candle holder. Red: $10-12 each. Imported for 'Design House' of Fort Worth, Texas (c. 1977); part of a three-piece set with 5", 7.5", and 9" candle holders. The glass is somewhat heavier than that of **Morgantown**.

McKee 6.25" x 5.75" 'Louvre' double light candle holder with pheasant in relief on center panel. Crystal with satin back panel, crystal satin: $140-150 pair. Hard to find.

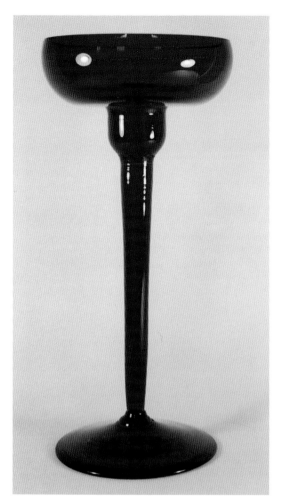

Mexico 9" single light candle holder.
Red: $10-12 each.

Mexico 13" single light candlestick. Crystal with gold twist: $20-25 each.

Mexico 7.25" single light candle holder. Crystal: $8-10 each.

Mikasa

Secaucus, New Jersey, 1948 to present. Design and marketing of tabletop products.

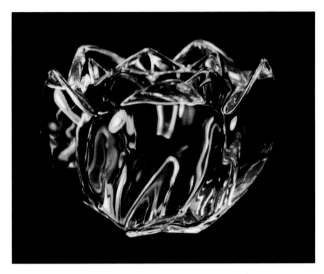

Mikasa 2.75" 'Solvenia' votive. Lead crystal: $8-10 each. Made in Germany.

Mexico 14" x 8.875" single light candle holder. Blue glass with light yellow drip plate, all iridized: $65-70 each.

Mikasa 5.25" domed single light candle holder. Crystal: $18-20 each.

Mikasa 5.75" single light candle holder. Crystal: $18-20 each.

Mikasa 6.75" single light candle holder with hexagonal base. Lilac: $25-30 each; lead crystal: $20-25 each.

Mikasa 9.5" single light candle pillar. Lead crystal: $25-30 each. Made in Germany.

Mikasa 5.25" single light candle holder with staked sphere column and base. Crystal: $18-20 each.

123

Morgantown Glass Works

Morgantown, West Virginia. Late 1800s-1903, became **Economy Tumbler Company**; 1929-1937, became **Morgantown Glass Works** again; 1939-1965, became **Morgantown Glassware Guild**; sold to **Fostoria Glass Company** in 1965. Pressed ware, blown ware, and blanks for many other companies.

Morgantown 3.75" #9935 single light candle vase. Ruby: $30-35 each; peacock blue, gypsy fire, ebony, pineapple, bristol blue, moss green: $25-30 each.

Morgantown 3.25" x 5.75" #9928 'Flowerlites' single light candle bowl and 3.75" #9935 single light candle/vase. Peacock blue: $50-55 set. Add $7 for the flower frog.

Morgantown console with 3.75" #9935 candle holders and 3.75" x 8" #9928 'Flowerlites' bowl. Ruby: $75-80 set. Add $7 for the flower frog.

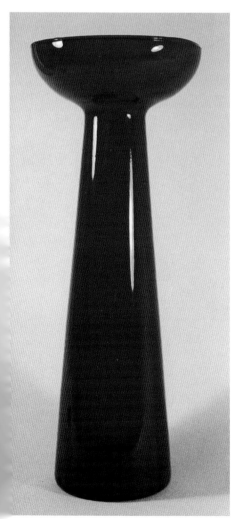

Morgantown 4" #2265 single light candle holder. Pink: $55-60 pair.

Mosser Glass Company

Cambridge, Ohio, 1964 to present. Pressed glass novelties and tableware.

Mosser 3" 'Dutch Boudoir' (old **U.S. Glass** mold) single light candle holders. Amber: $20-25 pair. (1980s-1990s). Marked on base.

Morgantown 8.5" #1200 single light candle holder/vase. Ruby: $40-45 each; peacock blue, gypsy fire, ebony, pineapple, bristol blue, moss green: $35-40 each. Also made in 5" and 7".

Mosser 3.5" single light fairy light. Amethyst with crystal base: $18-22 each. Marked on base.

New Martinsville

New Martinsvillle, West Virginia, 1901-1944. Sold and reorganized as **Viking Glass Company**. Innovative table lines and gift items.

New Martinsville 5" 'Moon Drops' single light candle holder. Crystal: $50-55 pair; amber, pink, light blue, dark green, light green, jade, amethyst, smoke, black: $60-65 pair. Ruby, cobalt: $110-120 pair. (c. 1932-1940s).

New Martinsville 8.5" x 12.5" #767 three light candelabra. Crystal: $45-50 each; amber: $55-60 each. (c. 1930s).

New Martinsville 6" double light candle holder. Crystal: $35-40 each. Used for plate etchings, especially 'Prelude.' (c. 1930s-1950s).

Paden City Glass
Manufacturing Company

Paden City, West Virginia, 1916-1951. Pressed
tableware and occasional ware.

Paden City 2.375" x 5" #701 rolled edge single light
candle holder. Cheriglo (pink) with gold inlaid etching:
$50-55 pair; crystal, pink, amber, green, ebony: $45-50
pair. Line #701 was produced in crystal and most of
Paden City's colors; additional colors are likely.

Paden City alternate view.

Paden City 2.375" x 5" #701 rolled edge single light
candle holder. Honey amber with floral decoration and
gold trim: $50-55 pair.

Paden City 2.75" #300 line #1503 single light candle holder.
Crystal with cranberry stain and cut-to-clear decoration: $40-45
pair.

Paden City 4" #412 'Regina' single light candle holder. Ebony: $75-80 each.

Paden City 6" line #555 single light candle holder. Crystal with 'Ardith' etching and gold trim: $30-35 each.

Paden City 5.75" line #555 single light candle holder. Crystal with silver deposit on the rings and medallion and cutting on the base: $25-30 each.

Paden City 6.125" "Butterfly" single light candle holders. Red (ruby) with unknown heavy silver butterfly-and-floral decoration: $95-100 each; crystal (found with deposits, etchings, or cuttings): $40-45 each. **Note**: This candle holder looks very much like a butterfly; and we have christened it accordingly.

Paden City close-up of 'Ardith' etching

Paden City 6.5" #116 single light candle holder. Amber, mulberry, blue, green (all with cutting or decoration): $75-80 pair; crystal with decoration: $45-50 pair. Also in 10".

Paden City 8.25" double light candelabra. Crystal only: $75-80 each. **Note**: Many attribute this to **Fostoria**; however the glass is different from most **Fostoria** items. We found this candelabra featured in an advertisement for an auction of **Paden City** glassware.

Paden City alternate view showing bobeche lip.

Paden City 6.25" x 7.625" line #890 'Crows Foot' triple light candle holder. Crystal with cutting: $40-45 each; Cheriglo (pink): $75-80 each; red (ruby): $95-100 each.

Paden City 6.25" x 7.625" 'Crows Foot' triple light candle holder. Red (ruby): $95-100 each.

Poland

Standard Glass
Manufacturing Company

Two plants: Bremen, Ohio, and Canal Winchester, Ohio. 1924 to present. Started as a subsidiary of **Hocking Glass Company**. Cut and etched tableware.

Standard 1.5" x 4" #852 single light candle holder. Pink with #901 floral cutting, green, topaz, crystal: $30-35 pair. (c. 1920s).

Poland 8.75" triple light candle holder. Lead crystal with bird motif: $45-50 each.

Standard 2.75" #833 single light candle holder. Green with #1100 'Xavier' cutting, yellow, crystal, pink, topaz: $85-90 each. (c. 1920s).

Taiwan

Tiara Exclusives

Dunkirk, Indiana, 1970-1998. A spin-off of **Indiana Glass Co.** Decorative and tableware items.

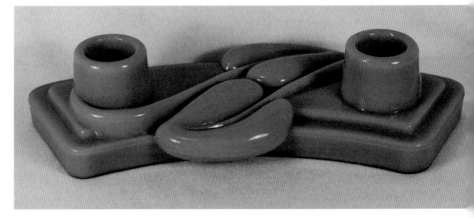

Tiara Exclusives (made by **Fenton**) 1.5" x 8.5" 'Desert Blossom' double light candle holder. Sage mist: $25-30 each; crystal: $20-25 each. Part of a garden center.

Taiwan 6.875" single light angel candle holder. Crystal with satin wings: $15-20 each.

Tiara Exclusives 3" single light candle holder (**Fenton** 'Water Lily' mold). Provincial blue opalescent: $25-30 pair; white lace crystal: $15-20 pair.

Tiara Exclusives (made by **Fenton**) 3.75" 'Desert Blossom' single light candle holder. Sage mist: $55-60 pair. This is the same mold as **Indiana's** 'Sunset Leaf' made in amberina.

Tiara Exclusives 1.625" x 2.75" single light press-cut candle bowl. Black: $20-25 pair.

Tiara Exclusives (made by **L.E. Smith**) 4" single light tri-panel candle lamp/votive. Pink with bird and floral motif: $15-20 each.

Tiara Exclusives 7.25" single light candlestick. Crystal with fired on red: $25-30 pair.

Tiara Exclusives 7.25" single light candlestick. Lead crystal with fired on pink iridescence, lead crystal with fired on lavender iridescence, lead crystal with fired on gold iridescence; lead crystal: $20-25 pair. Lead crystal also comes in 5.5": $15-20 pair.

Tiara Exclusives 7.625" single light candlestick with eight applied prisms. Light cranberry iridescent: $20-25 pair.

United States Glass Company/Tiffin

Pittsburgh, Pennsylvania. 1891-1938, moved main office to Tiffin, Ohio; 1951-1969, **Tiffin Glass** was the only remaining factory; 1980, final year of production. Dinnerware lines.

Tiara Exclusives 7.625" single light candle holder. Lead crystal: $15-20 pair.

Tiffin 1.625" x 2.875" #12 single light low candle holders. Skyblue satin, black satin, red satin, amber (old gold), blue, green, canary, black: $50-55 pair. **Note:** Although #12 (1924-1939) and #13 (1924-1934) appear to be identical, #13 is actually 1.66" wider and 1.33" taller than #12.

Tiffin table center. 1.625" x 2.875" #12 single light candle holder and 10" #179 rolled edge bowl. Skyblue satin: $100-110 set.

Tiara Exclusives (by **Indiana**) 8.25" 'Sandwich' single light candlestick. Light green, amber: $25-30 pair.

Tiffin 1.625" x 4.25" # 310 'Bowman' single light candle holder. Black satin, bright pink satin, bright green satin: $55-60 pair. (1924-1934).

Tiffin: 'Bowman' console set with 1.625" #310 single light candle holders, 2.875" x 10" #310 bowl and 1.5" x 5.75" #9320 stand. Black satin: $170-180 set.

U.S. Glass 2.25" #345 eight-sided single light spiral candle holder. Apple green: $45-50 pair.

U.S. Glass #345 console set with 2.25" single light candle holders and 9" bowl and epergne. Apple green: $140-150 set.

136

U.S. Glass 2.25" #345 single light candle holder. Crystal with #6712 'Trojan' etching: $40-45 pair; green with etching: $55-60 pair. (c. 1926-1932).

U.S. Glass 3" 'Puritan' single light candle holder. Crystal with cranberry stain etched-to-clear: $40-45 pair; crystal, crystal satin: $30-35 pair.

U.S. Glass 3" 'Puritan' single light candle holder. Crystal with cranberry: $40-45 pair.

Tiffin close-up of 'Fontaine' etching.

Tiffin 3.25" #9758 single light candle holder. Twilite blue with 'Fontaine' etching: $265-285 pair; rose, green; $175-200 pair; crystal: $110-120 pair. (c. 1924-1931).

Tiffin 3.25" #348 single light candle holder. Topaz: $30-35 each.

Tiffin 3.25" #348 single light candle holder. Crystal with green enameled 'Oneida' etching, crystal with blue enameled 'Oneida' etching: $80-85 pair. (1927-1935). Also comes with platinum band.

Tiffin table center. 3.25" #348 single light candle holder and 11.0" #348 three-footed bowl. Crystal with green enameled 'Oneida' etching: $150-160 set.

Tiffin 3.875" #6037 'Modern' single light candle holder. Applied crystal candle bowl with Killarney green base: $60-65 each; crystal/Killarney green with 'Melrose' gold band and gold inlaid 'Melrose etching: $95-100 each; crystal/Killarney green with 'Grapevine' gold and enamel: $75-80 each. (c. 1948-1950s). Signed.

Tiffin (from an old **Duncan-Miller** mold) 4" #741 'White Lace' single light candle holder. White milk glass: $35-40 each. (c. 1957). Formerly #121 line #41 'Early American Sandwich.'

Tiffin 5.875" line #17394 single light candle holder. Crystal. Killarney green: $80-85 each; pink with decoration: $95-100 each. Signed.

U.S. Glass 6.375" #56 Colonial style single light candle holder with hex-oval base. Crystal with silver deposit: $30-35 each.

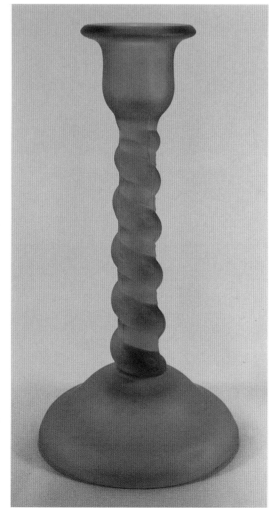

Tiffin 8" #66 spiral single light candle holder. Made in clear and satin colors. Royal blue: $60-65 each; amethyst, black: $45-50 each; canary: $40-45 each; emerald green: $35-40 each; crystal: $25-30 each. Three-part mold. **Cambridge** has a similar candlestick made with a two-part mold.

Tiffin 8.125" #66 single light candle holder. Emerald green satin, amethyst: $85-90 pair; canary satin: $70-75 pair; reflex green satin: $75-80 pair. Amberina; amberina satin: $80-85 pair; royal blue: $95-100 pair. (1920s-1930s).

141

U.S. Glass 8" #15328 'Brilliancy' single light candle vase. Reflex green, canary: $125-135 pair; amber: $100-110 pair; sky blue: $150-160 pair. (c. 1926-1930s). Three-part mold with six-panel candle cup.

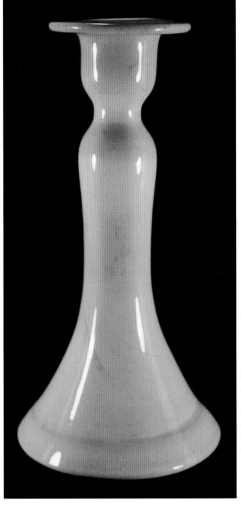

U.S. Glass 8.375" #151 single light candlestick. Jade green, pearl blue: $140-150 pair; coral red: $160-175 pair. (Introduced in 1921). Two-part mold.

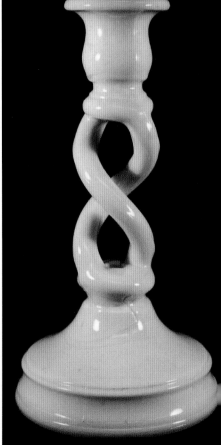

Tiffin 8.25" #80 single light open-twisted candlestick. White milk glass, jasper (opaque with reds, yellows, and browns), royal blue, blue, amber, amethyst: $100-110 pair; crystal with ruby stain: $115-125 pair; crystal: $85-90 pair. (c. 1920s).

Tiffin 9.25" #65 single light candlestick. Crystal with marigold iridescence: $95-100 pair.

Tiffin 9.25" #65 single light candlestick. Blue stretch: $150-160 pair.

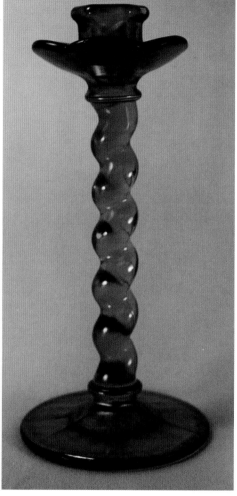

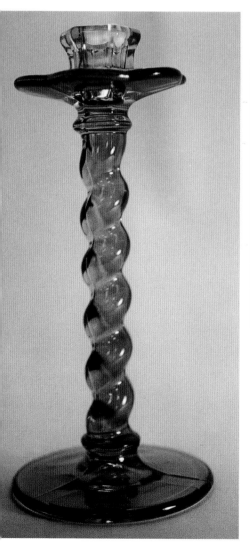

Tiffin 9.25" #65 single light candlestick. Crystal with amethyst iridescent stain, crystal with grey iridescent stain: $140-150 pair; crystal iridescent: $90-100 pair; crystal with fired on orange: $75-80 pair; crystal with fired on pink: $85-90 pair; blue stretch, topaz stretch: $150-160 pair. (c. 1922).

U.S. Glass close-up of bird and floral decoration.

U.S. Glass 10" #74 single light candlestick. Canary satin with heavy gold 'Enc. A-1' decoration, blue satin, jasper satin, black stipple, red stipple, peach blo, royal blue, light green, dark green, amber (also without decoration): $115-125 pair. (1924-1935). Paper label. Part of the 'Ritz-Carlton Assortment.'

U.S. Glass 10" #84 single light candlestick. Crystal satin with hand painted bird and floral decoration, green satin: $110-120 pair.

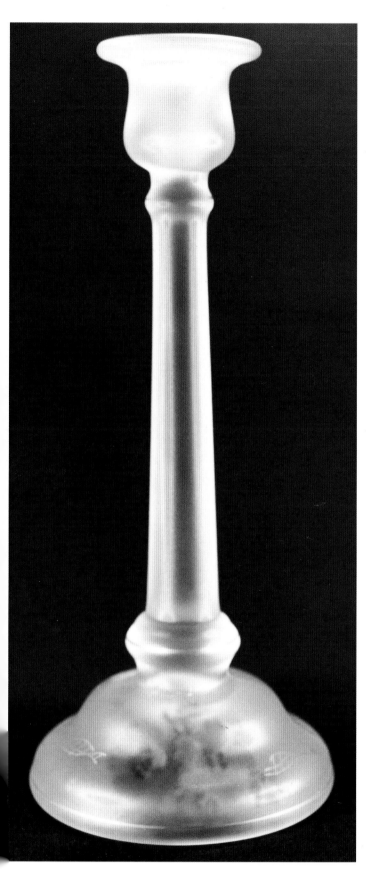

Tiffin 10.125" #84 single light candlestick. Crystal satin with hand painted floral decoration: $110-120 pair. (1920s).

U.S. Glass/Tiffin 8.75" #300 single light candlestick. Royal blue satin, black satin with gold decoration, green satin: $115-125; amber satin: $100-110 pair. (1920s).

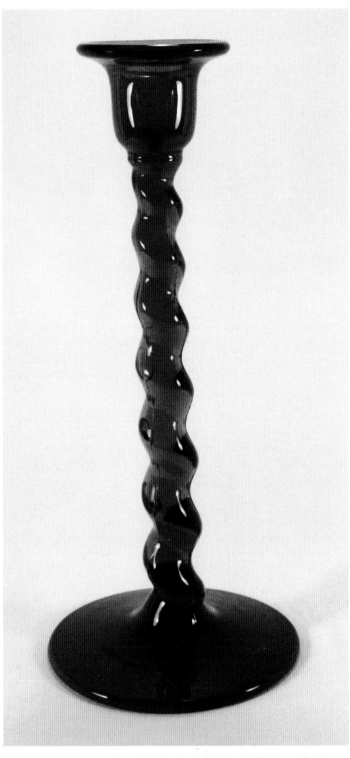

Tiffin 9.375" #315 single light candlestick with flat base. Red-orange with satin base, amberina satin: $100-110 pair; canary satin, sky blue satin: $120-130 pair; black satin: $90-100 pair. (1920s-1930s).

Tiffin 10" #319 single light candlestick. Sky blue with enamel and gold trim: $175-200 pair; black satin with enamel and gold trim, crystal satin with ruby stain: $150-175 pair; black satin with heavy gold trim: $125-150 pair; amberina satin with silver deposit: $295-315 pair.

Tiffin 10.25" #320 or #15320 single light candlestick. Black with "Myrtle' gold band and trim, black satin with enamel decoration: $125-150 pair; crystal; crystal satin, black satin: $100-125 pair; black with 'Eches' decoration $160-175 pair; ruby with 'Kimberly' decoration: $300-350 pair. (1920s-1930s).

Tiffin 10" #15179 single light candlestick. Royal blue, black, decorated satins: $300-325 pair; crystal with various decorations: $150-175 pair.

Tiffin #15179 or #179 console set with 10" candlesticks and 10" console bowl. Royal blue: $450-475 set.

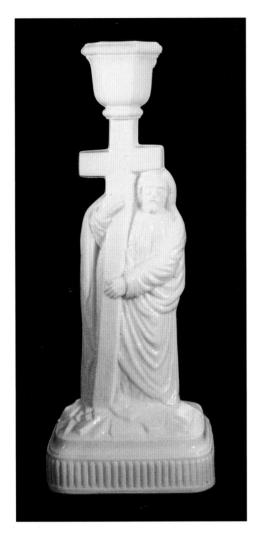

U.S. Glass 10.625" 'Crucifix' single light candlestick. Opalescent (white milk glass), turquoise (opaque blue): $250-275 each. (c. 1891). Found in *1891 Factory C Catalog.* Factory C was Challinor, Taylor & Co.

U.S. Glass 10.625" 'Crucifix' single light candlestick. Crystal (rare): $300-325 each. (c.1891). Found in *1891 Factory C Catalog.* Factory C was Challinor, Taylor & Co.

Tiffin 3.125" x 9.75" 'Lancelot' double light candle holder. Crystal: $30-35 each; green, citron: $40-45 each. This is a Pipsan-Saarinen-Swanson design. (c. 1949).

U.S. Glass 5" #15360 double light candle holder. Crystal with unknown cutting: $35-40 each. (1920s-1940s).

U.S. Glass 6" #15360 or #8220 triple light candelabra. Crystal with unknown cutting: $45-50 each. (1920s-1940s).

Tiffin 6.5" 'Williamsburg Pattern' triple light candelabra. Crystal with large floral etching: $45-50 each.

149

Viking Glass Company

New Martinsville, West Virginia, 1944-1986; 1987-1998, operated as **Dalzell-Viking Glass Company**. Popular modern glass.

Verleys

Originated in France in 1931. **Verleys of America, Inc.** (1935-1951) was established in Newark, Ohio, as a subsidiary of **Holophane Lighting Company, Inc.** (1935-1940). Colored pieces only were made from 1955-1957 with some molds being leased to **Heisey**. All molds were sold to **Fenton Art Glass Company** in 1966. Etched, cut, and buffed decorative glass.

Viking 3.75" #1507 'Epic' candle/flower frog. Green, blue, amber, orange: $30-35 each. (1960s).

Verleys 2.5" x 5.5" 'Water Lily' single light candle holder. Crystal etched: $40-45 pair; opalescent (milky white to pale blue with lots of fire), amber (translucent yellow), topaz (smokey grey brown), directorire blue (bright royal blue), dusty rose (applied pink with red overtones; rare): $90-95 pair. (1936-1951). Part of a three-piece console set. Not marked; paper **Verleys** label; paper labels were used to denote seconds. Mold is of French origin.

Viking 4.75" fairy light. Green, blue, amber, orange: $35-40 each.

Viking 6.625" #7600 line
'Cabbage Leaf' single light fairy
light. Orange: $35-40 each.

Viking 7" candle/flower frog. Amber: $35-40 each.

Viking 6.25" 'Epic' (#1287 **New Martinsville)**
single light candle holder. Grey-smoke, amethyst:
$40-45 each; crystal: $30-35 each. Originally sold
with a 10" globe as a hurricane lamp. (c. 1957).

Vineland Flint Glass Works

Vineland, New Jersey, 1887-1931. Owner created
Durand Art Glass Division in 1924-1931. Glassware,
tableware, lighting, and stretch glass.

Vineland Flint Glass 6.75" single light
candlestick. Tut blue, tut blue iridescent, wisteria,
dark wisteria iridescent, light wisteria iridescent:
$40-45 each; dark amber: $25-30 each; amber
iridescent: $30-35 each. (c. 1920s).

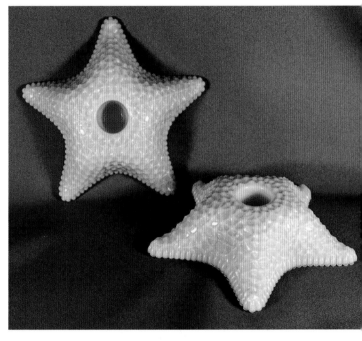

Westmoreland Specialty Company

Grapeville, Pennsylvania, 1889-1984. Milk glass
and giftware.

Westmoreland 1.375" x 5.25" SF-1 line #1063 'Starfish' single
light candle holder. Almond, antique blue, antique blue mist: $60-
65 pair. Milk glass mother of pearl: $50-55 pair; milk glass: $40-
45 pair; crystal mist: $35-40 pair. (c. late 1970s).

Westmoreland 2.75" single light
candle holders. Crystal with spray
cased green with gold decoration:
$20-25 pair; amber with cutting:
$25-30 pair. **Note**:
Westmoreland, **Fostoria**, and
others used this cutting.

Westmoreland 2.875" #1921/10 'Lotus' single light candle holders. Flame (amberina) (1967 only): $55-60 pair; golden sunset (amber), apricot mist, Bermuda blue: $40-45 pair; pink opalescent: $45-50 pair; green mist, light blue mist: $35-40 pair; olive green: $25-30 pair.

Westmoreland 3.75" #1921/2 'Lotus' low single light candle holder. Green mist (satin glass), dark blue mist, light blue mist, mother of pearl: $30-35 each; apricot mist, pink mist, lilac mist, pink pastel, pink opalescent: $35-40 each; black milk glass: $40-45 each; crystal with ruby stain: $45-50 each; flame: $55-60 each; crystal mist, white milk glass, moss green, golden sunset: $25-30 each; any spray cased color combination: $50-55 each. First introduced in the 1920s and produced intermittently until 1984. This 'Lotus' candle holder is currently being reproduced by **Fenton**.

Westmoreland 3" #1872-3 single light candle holder. White milk glass with 'Palm Tree' decoration, any decoration: $70-75 pair; any color without decoration: $45-50 pair. Reissued by Westmoreland in many colors; older versions are usually milk glass or crystal mist. **Summit Art Glass** currently owns the mold.

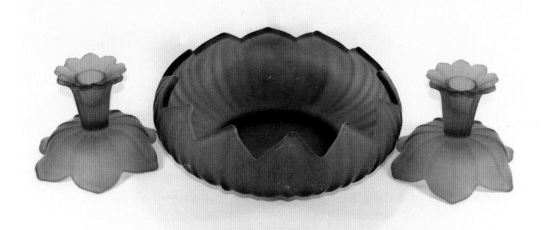

Westmoreland three-piece 'Lotus' console set. 3.75" low single light candle holder. Bowl 9". Green mist (satin glass): $95-110 set.

153

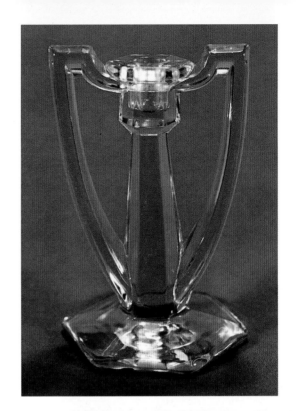

Westmoreland 3.75" #8 'Old Quilt' line #500 single light candle holder. White milk glass with 'Forget-Me-Not' decoration and gold trim: $65-70 pair; white milk glass: $25-30 pair. This decoration is found only on 'Old Quilt,' and very few pieces have gold trim. Scarce.

Top right: **Westmoreland** 4.5" #1015 'Childs Trophy' single light candle holder. Crystal: $55-60 each. (c. 1910-1930). Also comes in 6".

Westmoreland 5.75" line #1912 'Maple Leaf' single light candle holder with crimped top. Lilac opalescent, ruby: $65-70 pair; blue pastel, pink pastel, white milk glass: $35-40 pair. Introduced in the 1920s as 'Bramble,' it was reissued as 'Maple Leaf' in white milk glass in the 1950s.

Westmoreland 3" #1067/1 'Three Ball' candle holders. Blue, multicolor (crystal with flashed ruby, gold and blue), teal: $60-65 pair; crystal: $45-50 pair. Introduced in 1927.

Westmoreland 5" 'Maple Leaf' single light candle holder with a flat top. Black milk glass, white milk glass, mint green: $75-80 pair. Marked 'WG'. Black milk glass and cobalt are reportedly reproductions, although the black candle holders often carry the **Westmoreland** mark. The mold is currently owned by **Plum Glass**; their products are marked with a keystone 'P'.

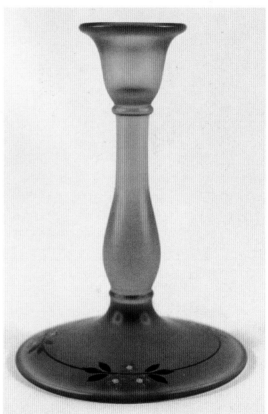

Westmoreland 6.25" single light candlestick. Amber satin with #119 blue enamel floral decoration: $40-45 each. (c. 1920s).

Westmoreland 'Maple Leaf' table center with 5" candle holders basket. Black milk glass: $150-160 set. **Note**: the basket is not from a **Westmoreland** mold.

Westmoreland 7"
#1007 single light
candlestick. Crystal only:
$45-50 pair; crystal with
decoration: $55-60 pair.
Also comes with painted
on decoration. (c. 1910-
1940). This is one of
Westmoreland's oldest
candlesticks.

Below: **Westmoreland**
7.375" #1012 single light
candlestick. Crystal with
heavy, deep cutting: $100-
125 pair. (1915-1925).

Westmoreland 6.5" #1042 single light candle holder.
Crystal with spray cased amethyst and Charles West's
patented #314 lattice design in gold, any color with
decoration or cutting: $40-45 each; any color without
decoration or cutting: $30-35 each. (c. 1920s).

Westmoreland console with 6.5" single light candle holders and 8" bowl. Crystal
with spray cased amethyst and Charles West's patented #314 lattice design in gold:
$140-150 set.

Westmoreland
8" #1012 single light candlestick. Crystal with cutting: $85-90 pair. (1915-1925).

Westmoreland
7.5" single light candle pillar. Crystal with cutting on column: $85-90 pair. (1915-1925).

Westmoreland
alternate view.

Westmoreland 7.5" #1016 'Paul Revere' six-sided single light candlestick. Crystal with cut flower design: $135-145 pair; plain crystal: $110-120 pair. (1911-1940). Also in 7": $100-110 pair; 7.5", 8", and 8.25": $115-125 pair.

Westmoreland 8.75" #1041 single light candlestick. Crystal with spray cased white and black with blue and gold hand decoration: $75-80 each. (c. 1930s).

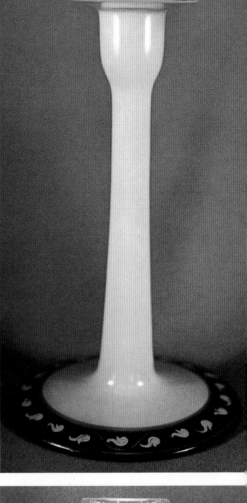

Westmoreland console set with 8.75" #1041 single light candlesticks and 4" x 10.25" bowl. Crystal with fruit and leaves painted on the underside then spray cased (reverse painting) with gold trim on top of the glass. Candle holders: $75-80 each; console set: $225-250.

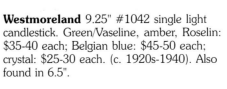

Westmoreland console set, alternate view.

Westmoreland 9.25" #1042 single light candlestick. Green/Vaseline, amber, Roselin: $35-40 each; Belgian blue: $45-50 each; crystal: $25-30 each. (c. 1920s-1940). Also found in 6.5".

Westmoreland 6.5" #68 'English Hobnail Line #555 double light candlestick. Crystal, opalescent (milk glass): $85-90 pair. (c. 1930s-1970s). **Note: Westmoreland** used the term opalescent for milk glass prior to World War II.

Yugoslavia 2.125" 'Troy Collection' single light candle holder. Crystal: $8-12 pair. (1990s).

Westmoreland 5" x 8" #26 line #1921 'Lotus' triple light candle holder. Crystal with pearlized spray cased finish of white, blue, and yellow, any spray cased color combination: $70-75 each; crystal, crystal mist: $30-35 each; light blue mist, green mist, pink mist, milk glass: $40-45 each.. Introduced in the 1920s; reissued in 1950s. Cased colors are scarce in this line.

Westmoreland white 'Lotus' triple light console set with 5" x 8" candle holders and 12.25" x 11" bowl. Crystal with pearlized spray cased finish of white, blue, and yellow: $200-225 set.

Bibliography

Archer, Margaret and Douglas. *Imperial Glass*. Paducah, Kentucky: Collector Books, 1978.

——. *The Collector's Encyclopedia of Glass Candlesticks*. Paducah, Kentucky: Collector Books, 1983.

Baker, Gary E., et. al. *Wheeling Glass 1829-1939 Collection of the Oglebay Institute Glass Museum*. Wheeling, West Virginia: Oglebay Institute, 1994.

Bickenheuser, Fred. *Tiffin Glassmasters (1929-1941)*. Grove City, Ohio: Glassmasters Publications, 1979.

——. *Tiffin Glassmasters Book II (1920-1950)*. Grove City, Ohio: Glassmasters Publications, 1981.

——. *Tiffin Glassmasters Book III (1915-1980)*. Grove City, Ohio: Glassmasters Publications, 1985.

Bones, Frances. *Fostoria Glassware 1887-1982*. Paducah, Kentucky: Collector Books, 1999.

Bredehoft, Neila. *The Collector's Encyclopedia of Heisey Glass 1925-1938*. Paducah, Kentucky: Collector Books, 1986.

Bredehoft, Tom and Neila. *Fifty Years of Collectible Glass 1920-1970 Volume II*. Dubuque, Iowa: Antique Trader Books, 2000.

Brookville Publishing. *Etchings By Cambridge Volume 1*. Brookville, Ohio: Brookville Publishing, 1997.

Burns, Carl O. *Imperial Carnival Glass*. Paducah, Kentucky: Collector Books, 1996.

Chiarenza, Frank, and James Slater. *The Milk Glass Book*. Atglen, Pennsylvania: Schiffer Publishing, Ltd., 1998.

Felt, Tom, and Bob O'Grady. *Heisey Candlesticks, Candelabra, and Lamps*. Newark, Ohio: Heisey Collectors of America Inc., 1984.

Florence, Gene. *Elegant Glassware of the Depression Era, Ninth Edition*. Paducah, Kentucky: Collector Books, 2001.

——. *Florence's Glassware Pattern Identification Guide*. Paducah, Kentucky: Collector Books, 1998.

——. *Florence's Glassware Pattern Identification Guide II*. Paducah, Kentucky: Collector Books, 2000.

——. *Collectible Glassware From the 40s, 50s, 60s... Fourth Edition*. Paducah, Kentucky: Collector Books, 1998.

——. *Collector's Encyclopedia of Depression Glass, Thirteenth Edition*. Paducah, Kentucky: Collector Books, 1998.

——. *Glass Candlesticks of the Depression Era*. Paducah, Kentucky: Collector Books, 2000.

Garrison, Myrna and Bob. *Imperial's Vintage Milk Glass*. Arlington Texas: Collector's Loot, 1992.

Glass Collectors Press. Vol XII, No.5. Marietta, Ohio: The Glass Press, Inc., 1999.

Glass Collectors Press. Vol XII, No.6. Marietta, Ohio: The Glass Press, Inc., 1999.

H.C. Fry Glass Society. *The Collector's Encyclopedia of Fry Glassware*. Paducah, Kentucky: Collector Books, 1990.

Heacock, William. *Fenton Glass The First Twenty-Five Years*. Marietta, Ohio: O-Val Advertising Corp., 1978.

——. *Fenton Glass The Second Twenty-Five Years*. Marietta, Ohio: O-Val Advertising Corp., 1980.

——. *Collecting Glass Volume 3*, Marietta, Ohio: Antique Publications, 1986.

——. *Fenton Glass The Third Twenty-Five Years*. Marietta, Ohio: O-Val Advertising Corp., 1989.

Heacock, William, James Measell, and Berry Wiggins. *Harry Northwood The Early Years 1881-1900*. Marietta, Ohio: Antique Publications, 1990.

——. *Harry Northwood The Wheeling Years 1901-1925*. Marietta, Ohio: Antique Publications, 1991.

——. *Dugan/Diamond The Story of Indiana, Pennsylvania, Glass*. Marietta, Ohio: Antique Publications, 1993.

Heacock, William, and Fred Bickenheuser. *Encyclopedia of Victorian Colored Pattern Glass, Book 5: U.S. Glass from A to Z*. Marietta, Ohio: Antique Publications, 1978.

Hemminger, Ruth, Ed Goshe, and Leslie Pina. *Tiffin Modern Mid-Century Art Glass*. Atglen, Pennsylvania: Schiffer Publishing Ltd., 1997.

Kovar, Lorraine. *Westmoreland Glass 1950-1984*. Marietta, Ohio: Antique Publications, 1991.

——. *Westmoreland Glass 1950-1984 Volume II*. Marietta, Ohio: Antique Publications, 1991.

——. *Westmoreland Glass Volume 3 1888-1940*. Marietta, Ohio: The Glass Press, Inc., 1997.

Krause, Gail. *The Encyclopedia of Duncan Glass*. Tallahassee, Florida: Father & Son Associates, 1976.

Long, Milbra, and Emily Seate. *Fostoria Tableware, The Crystal for America 1924-1943*. Paducah, Kentucky: Collector Books, 1999.

——. *Fostoria Tableware, The Crystal for America 1944-1986*. Paducah, Kentucky: Collector Books, 1999.

Madeley, John, and Dave Shelter. *American Iridescent Stretch Glass*. Paducah, Kentucky: Collector Books, 1998.

Mauzy, Barbara and Jim. *Mauzy's Depression Glass*. Atglen, Pennsylvania: Schiffer Publishing, Ltd., 1999.

Measell, James. *New Martinsville Glass, 1900-1944*. Marietta, Ohio: Antique Publications, 1994.

——. *Fenton Glass The 1980s Decade*. Marietta, Ohio: The Glass Press, Inc., 1996.

——. *Imperial Glass Encyclopedia Volume II*. Marietta, Ohio: The Glass Press, Inc., 1997.

——. *Fenton Glass The 1990s Decade*. Marietta, Ohio: The Glass Press, Inc., 2000.

Measell, James, ed.. *Imperial Glass Encyclopedia Volume I*. Marietta, Ohio: The Glass Press, Inc., 1995.

——. *Imperial Glass Encyclopedia Volume III*. Marietta, Ohio: The Glass Press, Inc., 1999.

Measell, James, and Berry Wiggins. *Great American Glass of the Roaring 20s and Depression Era*. Marietta, Ohio: The Glass Press, Inc., 1998.

——. *Great American Glass of the Roaring 20s and Depression Era Book 2*. Marietta, Ohio: The Glass Press, Inc., 2000.

Miller, C.L. *Depression Era Dime Store Glass*. Atglen, Pennsylvania: Schiffer Publishing Ltd., 1999.

National Cambridge Collectors, Inc. *The Cambridge Glass Company 1930 thru 1934*. Paducah, Kentucky: Collector Books, 1976.

——. *The Cambridge Glass Company 1949 thru 1953*. Paducah, Kentucky: Collector Books, 1978.

——. *Colors in Cambridge Glass*. Paducah, Kentucky: Collector Books, 1984.

——. *Reprint of 1940 Cambridge Glass Company Catalog*. Cambridge, Ohio: National Cambridge Collectors, Inc., 1995.

Nye, Mark, ed. for National Cambridge Collectors, Inc. *Caprice*. Cambridge, Ohio: National Cambridge Collectors, Inc., 1994.

Over, Naomi. *Ruby Glass of the 20th Century. Book 2*. Marietta, Ohio: The Glass Press, Inc., 1999.

Page, Bob, and Dale Frederiksen. *Seneca Glass Company 1891-1983, a Stemware Identification Guide*. Greensboro, North Carolina: Page-Frederiksen Publishing Co., 1995.

"Pattern Glass Preview," Issue Number Four, 1185-A Fountain Lane, Columbus, Ohio 43213.

Pendergrass, Paula, and Sherry Riggs. *Glass Candleholders: Art Nouveau, Art Deco, Depression Era, Modern*. Atglen, Pennsylvania: Schiffer Publishing Ltd., 2001.

Pina, Leslie. *Fostoria Serving the American Table 1887-1986*. Atglen, Pennsylvania: Schiffer Publishing Ltd., 1995.

——. *Popular '50s and '60s Glass*. Atglen, Pennsylvania: Schiffer Publishing Ltd., 1995.

——. *Circa Fifties Glass from Europe & America*. Atglen, Pennsylvania: Schiffer Publishing Ltd., 1997.

——. *Depression Era Glass by Duncan*. Atglen, Pennsylvania: Schiffer Publishing Ltd., 1999.

Pina, Leslie, and Jerry Gallagher. *Tiffin Glass 1914-1940*. Atglen, Pennsylvania: Schiffer Publishing Ltd., 1996.

Riggs, Sherry, and Paula Pendergrass. *20th Century Glass Candle Holders: Roaring 20s, Depression Era, & Modern Collectible Candle Holders*. Atglen, Pennsylvania: Schiffer Publishing, Ltd., 1999.

The Sandwich Historical Society. *The Sandwich Glass Museum Collection*. Sandwich, Massachusetts: The Sandwich Glass Museum, 1969.

Snyder, Jeffrey B. *Morgantown Glass: From Depression Glass Through the 1960s*. Atglen, Pennsylvania: Schiffer Publishing Ltd., 1998.

Stout, Sandra McPhee. *The Complete Book of McKee Glass*. North Kansas City, Missouri: Trojan Press, Inc., 1972.

——. *Depression Glass III*. Des Moines, Iowa: Wallace-Homestead Book Company, 1976.

Teal Ron Sr. *Tiara Exclusives Company Catalog Reprints*. Marietta, Ohio: The Glass Press, 2000.

Truitt, Robert and Deborah. *Collectible Bohemian Glass 1915-1945, Volume II*. Kenington, Maryland: B&D Glass, 1998.

Walk, John. *The Big Book of Fenton Glass 1940-1970*. Atglen, Pennsylvania: Schiffer Publishing Ltd., 1998.

Whitmeyer, Margaret and Kenn. *Fenton Art Glass Patterns 1939-1980*. Paducah, Kentucky: Collector Books, 1999.

——. *Fenton Art Glass 1907-1939*. Paducah, Kentucky: Collector Books, 1996.

Wilson, Chas West. *Westmoreland Glass*. Paducah, Kentucky: Collector Books, 1996.